CW00924955

Class 37

Crossing the infant River Test on Hurstbourne Viaduct in Hampshire on 26 September 1987 is No 37 116 in non-standard 'large logo' livery. The special, comprising Network SouthEast Mk 1 coaches, was working on the up road from Andover Junction in conjunction with 'Basingstoke 150', an event attended by thousands of railway enthusiasts. The Test meanders gently towards the coast, finally emptying into Southampton Water. *Author*

One of the attractions of the Class 37 is the glorious sound emitted from its 12-cylinder English Electric diesel engine, surpassed only by the larger 16-cylinder unit as used in the Class 50. Storming the climb towards Liskeard, Cornwall, at 18.46 on 12 September 1995 is St Blazey's No 37 671 *Tre Pol and Pen* with the weekly Ponsandane–Tavistock Junction empty tanks. The setting sun illuminates the sides of the *ensemble*, which was running 1¼ hours early; had the train been on time darkness would have fallen before this point was reached! On the right of the picture can be seen Liskeard's down advance starting signal. *Author*

Diesel Retrospective

Class 37

John Vaughan

Ian Allan
PUBLISHING

Contents

Introduction

At the time the British Railways Modernisation Plan evolved during the mid-1950s investment in diesel and electric motive power was paramount. The railways were still suffering from years of decline that had started with the advent of World War 2 in 1939. Some steam locomotives in daily operation dated back to Victorian times and the vast number of disparate types and classes reflected the many pre-Grouping and pre-Nationalisation railway companies.

Some attempt at standardisation had been made during the 1950s, resulting in what were broadly described as BR Standard steam locomotive types, but with modernisation, improved operating efficiency and a smokeless 'smog-free' environment all high on the agenda the end of steam traction was inevitable.

Experiences with diesel traction, particularly in North America, and with electric traction, in parts of Europe, had demonstrated that enormous cost advantages could be gained in modernising motive power, which brought with it greater availability, flexibility and reliability. Unfortunately although lessons on the way forward were being learned by the British Transport Commission it failed to take advantage of tried and tested diesel locomotive designs. In the United States of America many years of experience had culminated in some very robust diesel-electric locomotive designs, while in Germany diesel-hydraulic locomotives formed the backbone of non-electrified services.

In evolving a replacement for steam the BTC ignored established diesel designs from overseas and embarked instead on a course of experimental procurement which entailed ordering a wide range of varying and non-compatible diesel locomotives from a plethora of manufacturers. These featured various sizes and makes of power unit over a wide power range and coupled to a variety of transmission types. To be fair to the BTC there was enormous political pressure to 'buy British'. After the war British manufacturing was on its knees. Unemployment was high, significant investment through large orders was required and the thought of abandoning British industry and its skilled workforce by importing whole locomotives was politically unacceptable.

First published 2007

ISBN (10) 0 7110 3200 9
ISBN (13) 978 0 7110 3200 2

All rights reserved. No part of this book may be reproduced or transmitted in any form or by any means, electronic or mechanical, including photocopying, recording or by any information storage and retrieval system, without permission from the Publisher in writing.

© Ian Allan Publishing Ltd 2007

Published by Ian Allan Publishing

An imprint of Ian Allan Publishing Ltd, Hersham, Surrey, KT12 4RG

Printed in England by Ian Allan Printing Ltd, Hersham, Surrey, KT12 4RG

Code: 0706/B1

Visit the Ian Allan Publishing website at www.ianallanpublishing.com

No politician was going to retain his seat by advocating a policy of large-scale imports. It now seems almost ironic that from the late 1990s, some 40 years after the Modernisation Plan, the importation (from Canada) of powerful and efficient Class 66 locomotives is precisely what has happened!

British Railways' motive-power requirements were arranged neatly in power bands. It was envisaged that no fewer than 2,500 diesel locomotives would eventually be placed in service, but under a Pilot Scheme only 174 would be procured initially: 40 Type A (800–1,000hp), 106 Type B (1,000–1,200hp) and 28 Type C (2,000hp and over). Only 14 of the 174 locomotives would have hydraulic transmission. The BTC subsequently realised that these power bands were too narrow and restrictive, and they were later expanded to Type 1 (800–1,000hp), Type 2 (1,000–1,499hp), Type 3 (1,500–1,999hp), Type 4 (2,000–2,999hp) and Type 5 (3,000hp and over). Subsequently large orders were placed with a number of companies, English Electric and Brush benefiting most.

Here we are concerned only with the English Electric Type 3 Co-Co design, which was introduced at the end of 1960 and was later to become known as Class 37. English Electric had been at the forefront of British diesel-locomotive design, particularly with shunters before World War 2 and in main-line terms between 1947 and 1954, when five experimental diesel-electric locomotives were built for use on the London Midland and Southern regions. It was therefore logical that the English Electric company should receive a substantial slice of any cake that was on the table. The company was to be involved in many of the most successful locomotive types that emerged from the Modernisation Plan (particularly the 1,000hp Type 1 (Class 20), 1,750hp Type 3 (Class 37) and 2,000hp Type 4 (Class 40), as well as the 2,700hp Type 4 (Class 50) and the famous 3,300hp 'Deltic' Type 5 (Class 55). It made a significant contribution to Britain's railways in the 1960s and '70s, for example, eventually providing replacement engines for the Brush Type 2 (Class 30, later Class 31). Some of these locomotives have been so successful that nearly 50 years later many are

Above: A Class 37 as delivered from the Vulcan Works of the English Electric Co at Newton-le-Willows is represented by No D6711 in all-green livery with split roller-blind train-headcode boxes at London's Liverpool Street station during 1961. The first batch of 30 locomotives was allocated to East Anglia to replace steam locomotives and also to take over some services from less powerful Brush Type 2 diesels. *Ian Allan Library*

still in everyday use — a longevity that exceeds that of many classes of the supposedly more durable steam locomotive.

The original publicity material described the English Electric Type 3 (which will henceforth be referred to as Class 37) as a 1,750hp Co-Co diesel-electric to be built at its Vulcan Foundry. The blurb went on that the type was intended for mixed-traffic work but that with train-heating boilers and a maximum speed of 90mph they would be suitable for express-passenger services. It was further pointed out that the class could be operated in multiple with most other English Electric diesel locomotives of Types 1-4, which had a 'blue star' coupling code. The engine was simply described as an English Electric 12-cylinder 'V' engine rated at 1,750hp at 850rpm. This was capable of producing over 2,000hp but in the interests of reliability was rated more modestly for BR use. Initial deliveries were destined for the Eastern Region.

Few could have imagined the subsequent success of the class, and high availability figures were soon achieved. In total 309 locomotives were built between 1960 and 1965, and to speed up production they were constructed at both the Vulcan Foundry at Newton-le-Willows and at the Darlington works of Robert Stephenson & Hawthorn. The quoted weight ranged from 103 to 108 tons, depending on the precise

Left: Construction of the 309 English Electric Type 3s was shared between the Vulcan Foundry and EE's works at Darlington, previously owned by locomotive builders Robert Stephenson & Hawthorn. This stunning view, recorded during 1964 in the erecting shop at the Vulcan Foundry, shows no fewer than 11 Type 3s in various stages of construction. By this time the locomotives were being fitted with central headcode panels. *English Electric / Author's collection*

specification. Early locomotives had an 830-gallon fuel tank, a tank for boiler fuel and a boiler-water capacity of 800 gallons. There were six nose-suspended traction motors, one above each of the six axles, which each carried an (approximately) 18-ton load. The cost per unit was just over £83,000, English Electric benefiting from its use of major components across a variety of classes.

It would not be possible in the space available to provide a detailed history of all 309 locomotives that have worked over the majority of Britain's rail network for a period of 47 years, but there follows a brief summary of major developments. The locomotives have appeared in scores of colour schemes with variations not only in their primary colour but in terms of warning panels, size of BR arrows and locomotive numbers, depot repaints, various decals, logos, roofline and solebar stripes, marketing names and corporate styles. The main liveries are featured within these pages but obviously not every permutation could be included.

By the time the EE Type 3s were being delivered steam traction was in terminal decline, and the arrival of these reliable diesels with incredibly high availability figures (compared with steam) helped accelerate its demise. The first batch of locomotives was allocated to East Anglia in 1960/1 and was followed by batches for Hull Dairycoates, Darnall (Sheffield) and Thornaby (Teesside) depots. Hull and Darnall received further batches in 1962/3, as did Gateshead, while in the spring of 1963 there began a mass invasion of South Wales. From No D6755 only certain locomotives were fitted with train-heating equipment, because steam-heated carriages were in decline, and the facility was in any case not required on what was becoming mostly a freight-only type. (The absence of a boiler meant there was no requirement for a large water tank, and some locomotives were later fitted with 'long-range' fuel tanks, located where the boiler water tank was once situated, increasing fuel capacity to an impressive 1,689 gallons.)

From No D6730 all locomotives appeared from works with a small yellow warning panel on each cab end, reflecting a new BR safety requirement. Another change in appearance occurred when the cab end doors were deemed to be unnecessary, a consequence of this being the abandonment of the split headcode boxes in favour of a single, central headcode panel; this became standard from No D6819, the 120th locomotive delivered. (In later years these panels were plated over and marker lights fitted, and eventually all locomotives were fitted with a single headlight.) In the mid-1960s, following the widespread introduction of rolling stock and freight wagons with air brakes, significant numbers of Class 37s were also fitted with train air-braking equipment, which further broadened their operating scope.

Right: This profile shows the distinctive (if slightly dated) nose or bonnet of a Class 37, with hinged inspection hatches on the top. Also visible is one of the two Co-Co bogies with an electric traction motor driving each axle, using power generated by its 1,750hp English Electric diesel engine. No 37 175 was fitted with special bogies designed to reduce wheel-flange and track wear on tightly curved industrial sidings. Below the large number is a data panel (revealing, *inter alia*, that the locomotive weighs 105 tonnes) and a BZ (St Blazey) depot-allocation sticker. In 2006 this locomotive was moved to the Weardale Railway for preservation. *Author*

During 1965 some high-speed trials were conducted on the Western Region using pairs of Class 37s on Class 1 express-passenger trains. The locomotives put in some remarkable performances, especially when the 90mph maximum speed for the class was relaxed. However, although the trials were successful, the overall benefits were outweighed by the operational cost of running two Type 3 locomotives compared with that of a single Type 4. By the time the last EE Type 3 was delivered, late in 1965, the class was an established part of the national rail scene, and from 1966 some locomotives were reallocated to Scotland, with which they were to be associated for the next four decades; the same year saw plenty of other reallocation activity (particularly to the North East of England, where steam was soon eliminated) as new diesels came on stream.

During 1968 trials were briefly conducted using push-pull-fitted Class 37s for possible use on Glasgow–Edinburgh services, but in the event Type 2 (Class 27/1) locomotives were used. Although South Wales gave up some of its EE Type 3s they also commenced triple-headed services on Port Talbot–Llanwern iron-ore workings.

By the end of the 1970s the majority of passenger trains comprised electrically heated rolling stock, and many of the non-ETH Class 37s had been replaced on such duties. However, where steam-heated coaches were retained the members of the class still fitted with boilers were at a premium; well into the 1980s the class was employed on, for example, Liverpool Street–Cambridge trains as well as on many passenger services in Scotland. By 1979 the Class 37s had also arrived in Cornwall to replace less powerful and less reliable Class 25s, employed mainly (though not exclusively) on china-clay trains.

By the mid-1980s the class, which remained an essential part of BR freight services, had been in operation for more than 20 years, and a decision on replacement had become necessary. In the event it was decided to refurbish the class, replacing generators with alternators (in most cases by Brush) and providing lower-geared CP7 bogies. The first 31 locomotives so treated were equipped with electric train-heating (ETH) equipment and became Class 37/4s. Similar but without ETH and limited to a maximum speed of 80mph were the freight locomotives of Class 37/5, rebuilt thus from 1986. The opportunity was also taken to create a series of heavy-freight locomotives — Class 37/7 — with a starting ability equivalent to that of a Type 5; this was achieved by the addition of ballast to increase adhesion and tractive effort, overall weight increasing from about 105 to 120 tons, and

Left: Probably the biggest Class 37 line-up ever photographed by the author was recorded at the unlikely location of Chichester Yard in West Sussex on a Saturday in January 1994, by which time many Class 37s had been relegated from primary freight duties to British Rail's Departmental Sector. Having travelled from various locations, including Three Bridges, this impressive collection of track-panel and ballast trains was berthed in the up sidings in readiness for Sunday engineering work. On the right are Nos 37 194 and 37 293, while a Class 73 electro-diesel has slipped between the other two 'Syphons'. *Author*

route availability changing from RA5 to RA7. Eight of the '37/7s' were fitted with alternators by GEC (in lieu of the standard Brush equipment), while some were fitted with slow-speed control for use on 'merry-go-round' coal trains.

In the mid-1980s BR envisaged a new Class 38 freight locomotive of around 1,800hp, and during 1986 half a dozen Class 37s were selected for more extensive rebuilding, to act as component testbeds. Nos 37901-4 were fitted with Brush traction motors and a Mirrlees engine, while Nos 37905/6 received GEC traction motors and a Ruston engine. These weight-ballasted locomotives worked primarily in the South Wales Metals subsector.

Although the original intention had been to refurbish the entire class, the decision was taken to curtail the refurbishment programme in 1988 after 135 locomotives had been dealt with. However, this left a surplus of regeared CP7 bogies, which were then fitted to unrefurbished locomotives, creating the '37/3' sub-class.

Changes to BR's operating structure in the 1980s saw the creation of (among others) the Railfreight sector, which was to assume operating responsibility for the majority of Class 37s. In 1985 it introduced a new livery of grey with full yellow ends and a large BR logo (a scheme later modified by the addition of a red solebar stripe). Subsequently the desire for separate financial accountability saw Railfreight subdivided into a number of specific operating 'subsectors' pertaining to a major industry or groups of industries, and in 1987 it launched a new livery of three shades of grey with colourful subsector-identifying decals applied to the bodysides. By 1994 rail privatisation was on the cards, and three 'shadow' freight businesses — Transrail, Mainline and Loadhaul — were formed with a view to sale to different buyers; however, within a couple of years nearly all of BR's freight operations were sold to the Wisconsin Central Railroad of the USA, which incorporated the English, Welsh & Scottish Railway Co for its UK operations.

In the meantime, in the early 1990s, Class 37 withdrawals had commenced, due mainly to a decline in the volumes of freight traffic carried by rail and the delivery of Class 60s (and then, from 1998, General Motors Class 66 locomotives). A number of redundant Class 37s were adapted in 1994 for Sandite use, while in 1995/6, in readiness for the proposed introduction of 'Nightstar' services — sleeping-car trains connecting Channel Tunnel services with a number of British cities — a dozen Class 37/5s were fitted with compatible fittings and couplings for hauling such trains on non-

electrified lines. Ultimately the scheme collapsed, and in 1997 six of these locomotives, which had been reclassified as '37/6s', were acquired by Direct Rail Services (DRS), initially for nuclear-flask traffic; the other six passed to Eurostar, athough a further three would later find their way to DRS. During 1999 some 40 superfluous Class 37s were despatched to France to work engineering trains on the construction of a new high-speed line, while just over a year later a further 14 locomotives were transported to Spain for similar use. The latter were painted in a two-tone blue livery for operator GIF.

As the 20th century drew to a close, withdrawals increased apace, and many Class 37s started to be cut up. On the other hand many of the new, smaller operating companies, particularly DRS, actively sought these reliable locomotives. There were also pockets of passenger-train operation, mainly in North and South Wales, in Scotland and on the Settle–Carlisle line, but additional deliveries of Class 66 variants resulted in a further downturn in the ranks of surviving Class 37s. Gradually, the class was replaced on passenger trains, disappearing from North Wales by the year 2000 and the S&C in 2004 and relinquishing the majority of workings in Scotland during 2006, although a few continued into 2007. By this time EWS had a mere handful of operational machines but retained large numbers in store, both serviceable and unserviceable, at a variety of mainly northern locations. At the time of writing these venerable machines, in the hands of various operators, could still be seen at work in many parts of the UK on charters, SERCo test trains and a miscellany of freight workings, while a growing number are in operation on more than a dozen heritage railways nationwide.

To sum up, the Class 37s represent the best-value-for-money investment of any British diesel-locomotive design and have repaid their capital cost many times over. They are hugely popular with rail fans, and their good reputation is well deserved. This retrospective look at a remarkable class can do little more than give a broad but representative sample of the immense variety of operations over nearly half a century. I have experienced thousands of hours of Class 37 enjoyment all over the UK (but especially in Cornwall), and it is my sincere wish that this book give the reader similar enjoyment, while providing a huge dose of railway nostalgia. It is dedicated to my old friend Gavin Morrison, of Mirfield, Yorkshire, who has remained a loyal ally for nearly 30 years, and my thanks go to him (and to the other contributors listed in the Acknowledgements) for the assistance given with this book.

John Vaughan
Goring-by-Sea, West Sussex
March 2007

Great Eastern

Left: Class 37s have been associated with the lines of the former Great Eastern Railway for a staggering 45 years. The type arrived in quantity during 1961, and locomotives were soon displaying their mixed-traffic capabilities by working both express-passenger and freight trains. Among their last main-line passenger duties in the London area were Liverpool Street–Cambridge workings, largely on account of their steam-heating capabilities. On 25 February 1984 No 37 049 was 'steaming well' at Liverpool Street before departing for Cambridge. In 2006 Class 37s could still be found on Great Eastern lines in the London area, DRS examples being used in pairs on container trains to/from Ripple Lane. *Author*

Left: By the early 1980s electrification had reached only as far as Bishops Stortford, and Cambridge trains were all diesel-hauled. This typical scene from East London suburbia features split-headcode No 37 115 curving off the Cambridge line at Bethnal Green with a train for Liverpool Street; much of the old Great Eastern Railway infrastructure survives in the form of period awnings and an original GER station seat. The lines on the right run to Stratford, Colchester, Ipswich and beyond. *Author*

Above: This top-quality official British Railways photograph taken on 9 May 1963 shows the original English Electric Type 3, No D6700 (later No 37 119 and finally 37 350) at Dagenham with a special Ford Motor Company train to Halewood on Merseyside. By this time the locomotive had gained a yellow warning panel on each cab end. The view also shows the hinged nose-end access doors, which would later be deemed superfluous and overplated. *BR*

Below: On 29 December 1984 — a day when the murky weather resembled the London smogs during the age of steam in the early 1950s — miniature-snowplough-fitted No 37 031 in BR blue livery departs from the junction station of Stratford High Level with an up train of empty 'Cartics'. The lines visible to the left of the cab lead to Temple Mills Yard. *Author*

Above: A wintry scene on the Harwich branch at Bradfield, which although some 64 miles from London is nevertheless located in the county of Essex. On 12 December 1981 No 37 057 heads eight Mk 1 coaches forming a down Prins Ferries boat train from Liverpool Street to Parkeston Quay along the estuary of the River Stour, which at this point divides the counties of Essex and Suffolk. Class 37s shared these duties with Class 47 locomotives for more than three decades. *G. R. Mortimer*

Left: In the mid-1980s, before the line to Norwich was electrified throughout, there were a number of events that resulted in fewer appearances of Class 37s on Class 1 trains in East Anglia. In addition to the end of locomotive-hauled trains on the Cambridge line, the last locomotive-hauled service, by then reduced to morning and evening commuter trains only, between Lowestoft and London, was celebrated in 1984. Emerging from Ipswich Tunnel on 12 May is No 37 115 with the 17.00 Liverpool Street–Lowestoft. This last train carried Class 37 Preservation Society 'Farewell' and 'Broadsman' headboards, the latter proclaiming '1859 East Suffolk 1984'. *Author*

Left: This East Suffolk period piece shows a special military troop train from Newquay to Lowestoft passing Westerfield on 21 August 1966, behind green-liveried No D6720. The signal is 'off' for the Lowestoft line, whereas the other signal, controlling the Felixstowe branch, is 'on'. The special warning lamps beside the buffers were fitted experimentally to half a dozen of the class at this time. In later years Class 37s would pass this spot mainly at the head of Freightliner trains. *G. R. Mortimer*

Above: An East Anglian delight are the remains of the old GER Aldeburgh branch, which closed to passengers in September 1966. The line remained open for freight but in recent times has run only to a compound at Leiston, where nuclear flasks are transferred by road to Sizewell nuclear power station. Class 37/3 No 37 376 passes the old station at Leiston on 20 April 1995 with a flask from Willesden. The branch leaves the East Suffolk line at Saxmundham Junction. *Brian Morrison*

Right: The Port of Felixstowe has grown substantially over the decades due to a vast increase in container traffic. Although Class 47s and, more recently, Class 66s have handled the bulk of traffic, pairs of Class 37s have been regular visitors for a considerable time. Seen heading south from Derby Road station on 26 March 1988 are Railfreight-liveried No 37 043 (once named *Loch Lomond*) and all-blue No 37 128, with train 4Y68, the 04.28 Stratford Freightliner Terminal–Felixstowe North working. *Michael J. Collins*

Left: Shortly after the introduction of the first tranche of English Electric Type 3s (as the Class 37s were originally known) it became mandatory on British Railways for locomotives and units to carry yellow warning panels on all cab ends (a safety feature which would in due course give way to full yellow ends). Hull Dairycoates was an early recipient of the type, a dozen locomotives, Nos D6730-41, being allocated there from 1961/2. In this 9 June 1962 view at Hull Paragon No D6739 heads the prestigious 5.17pm express to King's Cross. Fish vans can be seen standing at the platform on the right. *Ian S. Carr*

Left: From their Stratford base the Great Eastern Class 37s worked a wide range of trains all over the network. Included in their duties were a number of oil trains working out of Ripple Lane. In this interesting picture an immaculate No D6726 speeds through Saunderton on the GWR's 'Birmingham Direct' route with the 4E08 Thame–Thameshaven train of empty petrol tanks on 18 March 1966. *H. K. Harman*

Left: In this incredibly rare photograph, taken on 5 February 1963, a shiny No D6744 leaves Chesterfield with the 1.28pm Chesterfield Central–Nottingham Victoria Class 2 stopping service. This train is running on the long-since-abandoned Great Central Railway route out of the city. Overlooking the scene is the Church of Our Lady and All Saints, which dates back to the 14th century and has a twisted spire that leans to the south, 9ft out of true. *D. Booth*

Above: Back in 1963 many routes of the former Great Central Railway had not been 'rationalised' and were still used by Class 1 trains. Not far from the preserved metals of the current GCR at Loughborough No D6744, one of the original batch of Type 3s delivered new to Sheffield Darnall in 1962, is seen again in smart green livery as it heads north with train 1N83 from Bournemouth to York on 8 June. Behind the driver's door can be seen the classic British Railways 'lion & wheel' symbol. *M. Mitchell*

Right: This scene, depicting a diesel locomotive in the steam age, was recorded at Retford on 21 May 1964. Having traversed the spur from the Sheffield line, No D6814, with a small yellow warning panel, pauses at the main line station with an old-fashioned Class 6 freight. The locomotive has been given 'the road', allowing it to propel its train back into the up yard. Visible on the platform is a wealth of wonderful railway infrastructure: old signs, 'flat hat' uniforms, barrows and the W. H. Smith's news stand. *Kenneth L. Seal*

Right: One of the most interesting long-distance Class 37 workings was the Manchester Piccadilly–Harwich service, for many years known as the 'Day Continental'. Diesel locomotives, which could be fuelled for hundreds of miles and run for days without significant servicing requirements, were ideally suited to the task. On 10 April 1964 1,750hp of English Electric power in the shape of No D6742 was made available for the 14.42 departure, seen here at Manchester Piccadilly. *R. D. Stephen*

Above: Recalling the days when substantial holiday traffic visited the Lancashire coast during the summer months, Railfreight-liveried Class 37/4 No 37 402 *Bont Y Bermo* (a name carried previously by No 37 427) reverses into Blackpool North before departing for Manchester Piccadilly on 20 July 1995. The locomotive had run round its incoming train in Blackpool North yard. Of note are the substantial signalbox, the semaphore signalling and, of course, the famous Blackpool Tower. *Brian Morrison*

Left: Another wonderful view of train 1E78, the 14.42 Manchester Piccadilly–Harwich boat train, this time on 2 June 1966 passing Godley Junction on the outskirts of Manchester, before tackling the Woodhead route over the Pennines. The locomotive, No D6701, is significant in having been the second of its type to emerge from the Vulcan Foundry, 5½ years earlier. The small onlooker will now be about 45 years of age. *F. Wilde*

Left: An unusual visitor to Stoke-on-Trent on 21 August 1984 was No 37 266, photographed emerging from the overall roof with an up empty-stock train comprising air-conditioned coaches thought to have originated from Longsight, Manchester. One thing is certain: the absence of passengers was fortunate in that this Class 37 could not have provided air-conditioning because it was a freight locomotive and not fitted with electric train-heating (ETH) equipment. *T. R. Moors*

Above: A powerful study in light and shade, greatly enhanced by the blast of exhaust, featuring 'large logo' Class 37/4 No 37 431 *Sir Powys / County of Powys* leaving Liverpool Lime Street with the 17.15 for Cardiff on Saturday 18 June 1988. The train will travel via Crewe, Shrewsbury and the North & West route through the Welsh Marches. Previously a freight locomotive, this Class 37 underwent ETH conversion in 1986 for use on passenger trains. *Gavin Morrison*

Below: One of the great railway hubs in the UK is Crewe, in Cheshire. Lines radiate in six directions, including the route to Chester and North Wales. In 1995 Crewe-based Class 37/4 locomotives took over certain North Wales services, a situation that continued until the year 2000. Although many of these were nominally allocated to the Provincial Sector they were owned by EWS, and some continued to carry pre-EWS freight liveries, such as Transrail. Rolling into Crewe on 14 July 2000 with the 10.07 Birmingham New Street–Holyhead is No 37 412 *Driver John Elliott. Brian Morrison*

Cambrian

Left: After a gap of some five years Class 37s returned to the Cambrian route west of Shrewsbury in 1986. The attractive original Railfreight livery of grey with large BR arrows and yellow ends, later modified by the addition of red solebars, suited the Class 37s. The repainting followed BR's move to a structure that involved the creation of various 'sectors' including one for freight. However, on summer Saturdays, when motive power was at a premium, it was not unusual for freight locomotives to be used on passenger trains. Such was the case on 16 July 1988, when this pair of Railfreight Class 37/5s was employed on the 09.40 Euston–Aberystwyth, seen in torrential rain near Talerddig. *Author*

Below: One of the Class 37s' regular weekday duties was powering the famous 'Cambrian Coast Express' between Euston and Aberystwyth, which travelled up in the early morning and down in the late afternoon. West of Shrewsbury the service was sponsored by the Provincial Sector, notwithstanding the use of InterCity stock. Coming off the single-line section and into the passing loop at Westbury, Salop, is No 37 429 *Eisteddfod Genedlaethol* with the up 'CCE' on 6 May 1988. The second man is leaning from the window in readiness to exchange single-line tokens with the signalman. *Author*

Right: The 11-coach 'Snowdonian', the 07.40 Euston–Pwllheli, is seen amongst the Welsh hills during its stop at Caersws on 16 July 1988. Whereas a single Class 37 was adequate for the six-coach 'CCE' these heavy holiday trains required double-heading, particularly on the return journey, with its steep climb to the summit at Talerddig. In appalling light and with marker lights glowing Nos 37 062 and 37 215 wait to depart for the Cambrian coast. Note the interesting mix of upper- and lower-quadrant signals; also the roofline stripe on the leading locomotive. *Author*

Right: Although general freight traffic disappeared from the Cambrian lines back in the 1980s one of the delights to survive was the Wednesdays-only fuel tankers to and from Aberystwyth. Although something of a safari to obtain, due to irregular running and a loosely observed timetable, a photograph of this train always provided satisfaction for the photographer. The train is seen leaving the Cambrian route and joining the North & West line at Sutton Bridge Junction, just south of Shrewsbury, in July 1991. Class 37/4 No 37 421 *Strombidae* was based at Immingham as part of the FPBI Railfreight Petroleum pool, so its allocation to this working was entirely appropriate. *Author*

Right: Typical Cambrian Coast scenery in the environs of Penrhyndeudraeth on 20 September 1986 as the 07.30 Euston–Pwllheli, headed by Nos 37 431 and 37 181, crosses the estuary leading to Traeth Bach. Beside the train is the old toll road that runs down to Harlech. For many years locomotives could run to Aberystwyth but not to Pwllheli because of a weakened weight-restricted bridge at Barmouth, some 17 miles to the south. *Brian Robbins*

Hope Valley

Left: The old Midland Railway Hope Valley route between Dore & Totley and New Mills in Derbyshire was a regular stamping-ground for Class 37s. The scenery along much of the route is spectacular, and Edale is the home of the Pennine Way. Here, on 4 June 1983, a 1,700-tonne double-headed westbound coal drag powered by Nos 37 226 and 37 209 passes Edale. Note the old steam-era 41A (Sheffield Darnall) shedcode plate on the front of the leading locomotive. The scenery in the background is typical Peak District. *Author*

Below: One of the staple commodities hauled by rail at the western end of the Hope Valley route has been limestone from the quarries in the Peak Forest/Great Rocks/Tunstead area. Mineral trains join the Hope Valley line at Chinley East and West junctions. With dust flying off a 1,900-tonne load of hoppers a train of 'Peakstone' passes the modern Chinley West Junction signalbox on 4 June 1986 behind Nos 37 229 *Cardiff Rod Mill* and 37 024. *Author*

Right: The long curve at Buxworth has been a favourite with photographers for many years. In delightful surroundings westbound HEA hopper wagons containing coal products run downhill behind Nos 37 215 and 37 132 on 17 June 1983. As built the Class 37s had a fuel capacity of 830 gallons plus 120 gallons of boiler fuel and a boiler-water capacity of 800 gallons, although in later years some locomotives were fitted with long-range fuel tanks utilising space vacated by the removal of the boiler-water tanks. *Author*

Below: Adding to the variety of Class 37-hauled trains traversing the Hope Valley route was the lengthy Cleethorpes–Manchester returning newspaper empties. Passing the derelict-looking platforms of the still-open Chinley station in 1984 is No 37 102. At 1961 prices the EE Type 3s cost just over £83,000 each to build, which would be about £2 million at current values. However, in terms of comparison with any other form of fixed business asset they have been a remarkable investment; few assets can be depreciated over a 40-year period! *Author*

Short Trains

Right: There is something amusing about a 1,750hp locomotive hauling a very short train, particularly when the train is shorter than the 61ft 6in length of the locomotive! In the first of four photographs featuring lightweight Class 37-hauled trains on the Western and Southern regions No 37 372, in original Railfreight livery but with red solebar stripe, hauls a single empty hopper wagon towards Didcot on the up road near Radley, south of Oxford, in July 1988. *Author*

Right: One of the most unfortunate reasons for lightweight trains is where the source of traffic is dwindling, leading in some cases to the complete withdrawal of the service. For many decades the consumption and distribution of household coal has been in terminal decline as the majority of households have converted to gas- and oil-fired installations. In May 1990, before the service was withdrawn, the returning Hove–Didcot–South Wales coal empties, comprising just a single wagon, is seen passing Pangbourne behind Railfreight Coal No 37 223 (with the subsector decal of black diamonds on a yellow background). Clearly this service was by then a loss-maker. *Author*

Left: Between 1986 and 1989, concurrent with the Class 37/5 conversions, a further 44 locomotives were converted for heavy-freight use by adding ballast to increase overall weight and therefore improve adhesion. These locomotives, forming the '37/7' sub-class, became Nos 37 701-719, 37 796-803 and 37 883-899. In July 1989 business was far from brisk for the Hamworthy–Cardiff Tidal Sidings service, seen passing Salisbury behind Railfreight Metals-liveried No 37 716. The extra ballast would be wasted on this working! *Author*

Left: Light work for a Class 37 on 29 March 1982, when old-fashioned brake vans still featured as part of the BR freight scene. Having visited Long Marston with an inbound load, No 37 188 is about to join the Cotswold route between Oxford and Worcester at Honeybourne. This locomotive was an example that retained a steam-heating capability for some time and saw service in South Wales, working out of Cardiff Canton. Note the lovely GWR signalbox and the semaphore signalling in the background. *Author*

York

Right: Although Class 37s were regular performers in the York area they were far more likely to be observed on freight workings using the avoiding lines rather than running through the station. An exception to the rule on summer Saturdays was a Glasgow–Scarborough (and return) working that was regularly Class 37-hauled. Here, having just reversed direction in York station, the returning 1S99 train is seen departing northwards behind No 37 108 of Eastfield depot, Glasgow; note the white West Highland terrier motif on the side of the locomotive. *Author*

Left: An impressive panoramic view of the entire area at York Yard North Junction on 26 May 1978. On the far left is the main line from Newcastle and Darlington, which curves to the left and then right on its approach to York station; threading its way through the Clifton area on the avoiding freight line is a down tanker train double-headed by Nos 37 079 and 37 007. Compared with the current railway scene the variety of railway vehicles in the background is nothing short of remarkable. *Gavin Morrison*

21

Cambridge Road

Left: As late as the mid-1980s the route from Liverpool Street to Cambridge was a delight to the railway enthusiast, for at that time it was still possible to travel in Mk 1 or early Mk 2 rolling stock behind steam-heat Class 37s (and a handful of Class 31s) past semaphore signals and, especially north of Bishops Stortford, sets of manually controlled crossing gates. An unidentified split-headcode Class 37 is seen arriving at Audley End from Cambridge in 1984. *Author*

Below: This charming, almost rustic scene shows Stansted station before the branch to Stansted Airport was opened. Speeding through the station in 1981 is a nine-coach express, the 16.00 King's Lynn–Liverpool Street, headed by a sparkling No 37 084. Although initially electrified only as far as Bishops Stortford the entire route was subsequently modernised and disfigured by overhead catenary, bringing to an end the era of diesel-hauled trains. *Author*

Above: In original condition BR green No D6721 storms past Trumpington signalbox, just a couple of miles from Cambridge, at the head of a down express comprising a rake of maroon-painted stock. In the 45 or so years since this photograph was taken the class has been subject to scores of liveries, including BR standard blue, 'large logo' blue, original Railfreight grey, British Steel blue, Railfreight triple grey (with various decals), Civil Engineer's 'Dutch', InterCity, Regional Railways, Transrail, Loadhaul, Mainline, European Passenger Services, EWS, 'Royal Scotsman' and DRS, not to mention hundreds of minor variations. Yellow paint has been applied in standard and non-standard styles, and stripes at solebar and roofline level have varied enormously; locomotive numbers have been large and small, as have BR arrows, whilst a multitude of transfers, motifs, marketing logos and depot plates have been applied in numerous different positions. *Ian Allan Library*

Left: Concluding this section featuring the Cambridge line is this vintage view of Cambridge North in September 1971, with a Class 8 Temple Mills–Whitemoor goods train trundling out of the station behind No 6744. In the background is a Class 08 shunting the extensive freight yard. After the end of steam the 'D' prefix to diesel locomotive numbers was dropped. Numbers were amended to the computerised TOPS system from 1973, when the class number was incorporated as a prefix to the locomotive identifying number. Thus No D6744 became No 6744 (as seen here) and then No 37 044 — and, later still, upon conversion in 1988 to a ballasted '37/7', No 37 710. *I. J. Hodson*

Standedge Route

Left: One of the most scenic stretches of railway line in the UK is the trans-Pennine route via Standedge and Diggle, which between Huddersfield and Stalybridge affords both train passengers and observers splendid views. There are impressive viaducts, and the climb on either side of the Pennines culminates in the impressive 3-mile 64yd Standedge Tunnel. Bursting out of the north tunnel, a grubby No D6717 passes through Diggle station (closed October 1968) with a rake of maroon Mk 1 coaches forming the Saturdays-only Morley Low–Blackpool North on 6 August 1966. *John Clarke*

Below: Daytime freight trains using the Standedge route in the 1980s were not especially numerous, among the few regular workings being the daily Haverton Hill–Glazebrook tankers and return. On 9 March 1985 the outward train was entrusted to No 37 140, seen here creeping through Stalybridge, which station was notable for its huge clock and a platform buffet/bar that sold excellent real ale. In later years the train was normally hauled by a Class 37/5, fitted with lower-geared CP7 bogies to increase haulage capacity. *Author*

Right: Seen in the deep cutting through rock at Springwood Junction, just to the west of Huddersfield, No 37 075 would have been on full power for the long climb up to Standedge with a heavy coal train in June 1983. Track rationalisation in the foreground is all too evident. Prior to the arrival in the late 1980s of Class 158 DMUs most passenger trains on this trans-Pennine route were locomotive-hauled, and with an hourly train in each direction — plus the occasional freight — this location was a photographer's delight. *Author*

Below: An order was placed in 1961 for a further 100 EE Type 3s, to be numbered D6819-6918. These were designated for freight duties only, and in consequence many were not fitted with train-heating boilers. Here one such locomotive, No D6878, crosses to the fast line at Heaton Lodge Junction with a freight for Huddersfield on 8 September 1967. Back in the 1960s the majority of the old Yorkshire textile mills had their chimneys intact, as seen in the background, but many have now been razed and the chimneys felled. *B. J. Ashworth*

Left: Winter has arrived in the Pennines as No 37 095 *British Steel Teesside* curves into Marsden on the Yorkshire side of the range with a block train of large ICI bogie tankers returning to the Middlesbrough area on 22 February 1986. This locomotive was then allocated to Thornaby and was fitted with additional fuel-tank capacity. The white upper-body stripe and 'Kingfisher' depot transfer were commonly applied to Thornaby's allocation of Class 37s. *Gavin Morrison*

Below: A magnificent afternoon vista on the Diggle route on 5 July 1983, with the splendid Saddleworth Viaduct being crossed by No 37 196 hauling coke from Healey Mills to Garston, on the banks of the River Mersey. The site of the closed Diggle station is at the upper left of the photograph. The train is vacuum-braked, but gradually the entire Class 37 locomotive fleet was converted to dual braking so that more modern air-braked freight wagons could be worked. Within two years this locomotive would be transferred to Cornwall for hauling china-clay trains, receiving the name *Tre Pol and Pen. Gavin Morrison*

Above: A charming scene recorded not far from *Last of the Summer Wine* country on 16 June 1983. The sound of the 12-cylinder English Electric diesel engine reverberates off the Yorkshire hillsides surrounding the eastern entrance to Standedge Tunnel as No 37 050 prepares to plunge into the 3-mile 64yd bore with a heavy westbound coal train comprising 20 HAA hopper wagons. Note the waterway, the canal basin and (right) the trackbed leading towards the abandoned bore of the south tunnel. *Gavin Morrison*

Left: Although Class 37s had featured on the Standedge route scene since their introduction it was always a pleasure to see the purposeful Type 3s pounding over the Pennines. Having emerged from Standedge Tunnel with a long vacuum-braked train of coke (the waste product of burned coal), No 37 165 enjoys the start of some downhill running as it heads west past Diggle Junction signalbox on 17 June 1983. The backdrop is spectacular, which is more than can be said of the modern housing development. Note the surviving semaphore signals on the right of the picture. *Gavin Morrison*

South Central

Left: The old London, Brighton & South Coast Railway lines, latterly known as the Central Division of the Southern Region, have never been noted for Class 37 infestation, but over the years there have been regular appearances on a few specific workings. Among these were the oil trains of the Railfreight Petroleum subsector, working out of Ripple Lane. In January 1993 No 37 892 *Ripple Lane* (formerly No 37 149) from the FPFR pool was photographed at Earlswood, south of Redhill, Surrey, with a train for the Cory sidings at Horsham, West Sussex. *Author*

Left: Class 37/7s Nos 37 883-899 were rebuilt concurrently with Nos 37 701-719, being given a higher number series simply because it was decided to maintain the distinction between the earlier (D6700-6818) and later (D6819-6999, 6600-6608) series. Here, No 37 890 is seen on another Petroleum subsector working but this time to the interesting location of Portfield, on the outskirts of Chichester, West Sussex. The freight siding, which, sadly, has now fallen into disuse, was a spur from the West Coastway line between Brighton and Portsmouth. However, in December 1990 business was brisk, with tankers belonging to the Shell Oil Company discharging their load into local storage tanks. *Author*

Left: Photographs of Class 37s on the Southern's Coastway lines have always been high on the 'required' list, and on 24 February 1990 an engineering possession of the London–Brighton main line afforded a rare opportunity. No 37 217 is seen passing the author's home station of Goring-by-Sea with the diverted 6V04 return working of the 03.30 Didcot–Hove coal train. Just four observers and the photographer were on hand to witness the event. Sadly this is yet another load that the railways have lost to road transport. *Author*

No fewer than four station signs identify the location as the seaside resort of Brighton. On 12 March 1983, Norwich City Football Club was playing Brighton & Hove Albion at the now-closed Goldstone Ground in Hove, and a Footex special was organised for the Norwich fans. The train was, surprisingly, worked throughout by No 37 092, resulting in a rare appearance of a 'Syphon' in the town. Having taken the fans to Hove station the locomotive was stabled at Brighton pending the return working. The cars in the background are parked on land (since redeveloped) that was once occupied by the long-since-demolished Brighton Locomotive Works. The locomotive was distinctive through having one headcode box filled in yellow and the other in black. *Author*

Bogie Tankers

Above: There have been radical changes in the oil-distribution business over the past 30 years, and the development of pipeline technology and the creation of networks has seen a major shift away from block trainloads of the precious fluid. Once capital expenditure on infrastructure has been discounted there are considerable economies and flexibility that can be achieved in pipeline distribution. Also, in the past, sometimes irresponsible industrial action by railway trade unions has affected supplies, a situation eliminated at a stroke by the use of pipelines. Heading up the local line at Pangbourne in May 1990 are Nos 37 248 and 37 273, bound for Langley with a load of 1,500 tonnes gross, probably from Milford Haven. *Author*

Left: A largely neglected stretch of line in terms of railway photography is the old GWR/GCR joint 'Birmingham Direct' route through High Wycombe in Buckinghamshire. Curving through the station at 18.10 on 3 June 1988 is a train of empty oil tankers returning from Thame to Ripple Lane behind No 37 709 (formerly No 37 014), which at that time was allocated to the FPLX (Freight Petroleum London) pool, based at Stratford depot. *Author*

Above: Westbury, in Wiltshire, is mostly associated with stone traffic from the quarries at Whatley and Merehead in Somerset. However, this 1983 scene features a brace of Class 37s in the form of Nos 37 276 and 37 279 heading through the junction station in the up direction with a train of bogie tankers – thought to be the Robeston–Theale oil. Over the years the Class 37s have been given numerous nicknames by younger railway enthusiasts, 'Syphons', 'Tractors' and 'Growlers' being just a few! *Author*

Below: Sporting blue-and-yellow Petroleum subsector decals on their Railfreight triple-grey livery, Nos 37 273 and 37 248 from the Cardiff pool approach Moreton Cutting, just west of Didcot, with a train of empties from Langley in May 1990. At one time there was considerable rail-borne oil traffic from the refineries at Robeston, Waterston and Milford Haven, but trainload petroleum from the surviving Dyfed locations now amounts to a fraction of the volume carried in earlier decades. *Author*

Welsh Valleys

Left: The Class 37s' association with South Wales has endured for more than four decades. Back in September 1962 Nos D6742 and D6743 were loaned to Cardiff Canton depot for evaluation and crew familiarisation pending the allocation of the type in large numbers. Cardiff's first example, No D6819, was delivered in March 1963, and the supply of new locomotives continued until November 1965, when No D6608 was received by Landore, Swansea; by this time more than half the fleet was based in the Principality. This atmospheric scene at an old-fashioned coal installation features Railfreight Coal No 37 698 *Coedbach* heading some vintage MDV wagons at Maesteg Washery in April 1989. Hopefully there were some sleepers somewhere under the coal dust! *Author*

Below: Although the class could be observed on the South Wales main line it was the sight and sound of 'Syphons' working in the confines of the Welsh Valleys that really excited. Unfortunately, over the past 30 years the Welsh coal industry has virtually disappeared, and scores of collieries have been closed. The steel industry has also declined with the closure of major plants. Seen amid typical Welsh scenery in April 1989, No 37 886 pounds up the Ebbw Vale branch with steel coil bound for the British Steel Corporation's Ebbw Vale tin works. This installation has now closed, and the line is currently mothballed; however, plans are in hand for the reinstatement of passenger services (after an absence of more than 40 years!), which could see the line reopen by the end of 2007. *Author*

Above: Business was very brisk at Ebbw Vale Steel Works on 17 September 1998 with dozens of wagons of steel coils and four Class 37s stabled in the sidings. The locomotives are in Railfreight, Transrail and Mainline livery, those nearest the camera being Nos 37 212 and 37 274. The other two locomotives are Class 37/7s, rebuilt in the late 1980s with additional ballast weight to improve adhesion and reduce the need for double-heading on heavy freights, including those to Ebbw Vale. *Gavin Morrison*

Below: Once upon a time just about every Welsh valley was served by rail, and in many instances there were competing railways on either side of a valley. The line depicted here was the old Rhymney Railway line from Ystrad Mynach to Dowlais (Cae Harris) via Nelson & Llancaiach, which closed to passengers in June 1964. When photographed in September 1986 the single line was used only by coal traffic from Cwm Bargoed, Aberthaw power station being the primary destination. Nearing Treharris are Nos 37 230 in standard BR blue livery and 37 505 in the original Railfreight scheme. *Author*

Right: The lines from Park Junction (near Newport) to Ebbw Vale, Rose Heyworth and Markham once served numerous coal mines, but gradually the industry was destroyed by a wider use of oil and gas, cheap coal imports, political dogma, geological faults and corporate economics. Many of the pits were household names in the valleys, and people's entire lives, from employment to education, housing and recreation, were dominated by the coal industry. In the postwar years pit closures accelerated, and by the 1990s the industry had been truly decimated. No 37 165 passes a scene of total dereliction at South Celyn Colliery, south of Aberbeeg, on 19 September 1986. The remains in the foreground would shortly be razed to the ground. *Author*

Below: The disappearance of the remarkable and unique coal-pit scenery of South Wales was a major loss to the region, bringing to an end a history that substantially pre-dated the Industrial Revolution. In this stunning vista, recorded in September 1986, Nos 37 698 and 37 239 leave behind the impressive Deep Navigation Colliery complex and make for Taff Merthyr Colliery with a long rake of empty HAA hopper wagons. Opened in 1873, Deep Navigation, known originally as Ocean Colliery, once employed 2,280 men and had a 10-mile underground railway network! During the 1980s annual output averaged 375,000 tonnes, but this would not prevent its closure in 1991. *Author*

Photographs taken only 20 years ago are now part of the rich history of the South Wales coal-mining industry and the railways that served it. Deep in Ebbw Vale was Marine Colliery, which in 1913 employed no fewer than 2,407 men. In 1927 there was a terrible disaster when an underground explosion took the lives of 52 men. It was integrated with Six Bells Colliery in 1970, but by March 1989 the entire complex had closed forever. Against an awesome industrial backdrop the crew of No 37 284 prepare to change ends during the run-round of its train of ageing vacuum-braked wagons. *Author*

Dutch Engineers

Above: Following the sectorisation of British Rail and with privatisation looming, Class 37s began to appear in a bewildering array of liveries. After a brief period when all-grey was used the Departmental Sector adopted a livery of grey and yellow which resembled that of certain locomotives in the Netherlands, and consequently the scheme became known as 'Dutch' livery. Taking a break from civil-engineering duties on a summer Saturday in 1992, No 37 197 passes the diminutive Thornford station (between Yeovil Pen Mill and Dorchester) with a train from Bristol Temple Meads to Weymouth. The coaches are painted in Regional Railways livery. *Author*

Left: 'Dutch' livery particularly suited the Class 37s, and the scheme is seen to advantage in this view at Lostwithiel in Cornwall. Tucked away in the up loop on 8 October 1993 is No 37 207 at the head of the down Dover–Goonbarrow 'Polybulks', which had travelled empty from one of English China Clay's Italian customers. The locomotive was then in the Civil Engineer's DCWA (Departmental Western) pool, based at Cardiff. Happily it is now preserved on the Plym Valley Railway in Devon. *Author*

Above: In June 1993 Nos 37 012 and 37 264, both unrefurbished locomotives and both in the DCWA pool, were fit for purpose and employed on precisely the type of train that they should have been hauling — a Civil Engineer's ballast train. The formation is trundling along the down local line at Moreton, just east of Didcot. The leading locomotive has had its nose-end doors overplated, although the split headcode boxes have survived. *Author*

Below: A pleasant rural scene beneath Surrey's North Downs at Ranmore Common, west of Dorking, features 'Dutch'-liveried No 37 377 heading west 'light engine' in November 1993. This locomotive was one of the Departmental Sector's few Class 37/3s, fitted with re-geared CP7 bogies. By 1992 as many as 35 Class 37s had been painted in grey and yellow, but the colour scheme would gradually disappear following organisational changes later in the decade. *Author*

Avon Calling

Above: One of the most remarkable episodes in the history of the class occurred in the mid-1960s, when the Western Region experimented with a pair of the Type 3 locomotives working in multiple on prestigious express trains. With a combined output of 3,500hp and a raising of the normal 90mph maximum speed they achieved some spectacular performances during 1965, including a journey from Bristol to Paddington in 86min 35sec and a Paddington–Exeter St Davids run in 132min 21sec, both being records. Speeds of over 100mph were recorded, but by mid-1966 such workings had petered out. Here, on 15 May 1966, Nos D6882 and D6881 are seen leaving Bath Spa with the 12.45 Paddington–Bristol Temple Meads. *Ian Allan Library*

Below: Compared with the history and grandeur of Bristol Temple Meads station Bristol Parkway is an architecturally depressing structure. To the west is a three-way junction where lines to Temple Meads, Avonmouth and South Wales diverge. Seen passing the two curved platforms in June 1990 is No 37 252, one of Tinsley's Railfreight Distribution fleet, with an up working of air-braked four-wheelers. Sheffield depots had a long association with the class, Darnall having received Nos D6742-54 in 1962. *Author*

On 1 August 1983 this wonderful array of semaphore signals was located at Hallen Marsh Junction, adjacent to sidings serving Avonmouth Docks, a Fisons depot, Commonwealth Smelting and an ICI plant. Having arrived from South Wales, No 37 204 sets about shunting its train while a privately owned Sentinel diesel shunter competes for attention on the left. Note, in the foreground, the extensive point rodding and the multitude of signal wires commensurate with manual signalling. This location can still be observed from branch trains travelling to and from Severn Beach station, but the semaphores are long gone. *Author*

Settle & Carlisle

Above: During the 1980s the scenic Settle & Carlisle line was threatened with complete closure. Opened for passenger trains in 1876, the Midland Railway's route to Scotland had been expensive to build and was costly to maintain. Closure was averted, but long-distance passenger trains from London and Nottingham to Carlisle and Glasgow were eventually withdrawn. The surviving Leeds–Carlisle service was provided mainly by DMUs, but there was some excitement in 2002 when Arriva Trains Northern announced that it would be running a locomotive-hauled service over the route using EWS Class 37s, which would normally top-and-tail four-coach trains. On a delightfully autumnal 17 October 2003 EWS-liveried No 37 405 pulls into Appleby station with the 13.44 Carlisle–Leeds. *Gavin Morrison*

Left: A glorious view on the Settle & Carlisle line at Armathwaite, towards the northern end of the route, showing to good effect the top-and-tail operation. No 37 408 *Loch Rannoch* heads the 13.31 Carlisle–Leeds on 13 November 2003. The Class 37/4s' ETH capability saw them widely used on passenger services including the West Highland line, the North Wales main line, the Rhymney branch and some Bristol–Weymouth services, as well as the S&C. *Gavin Morrison*

Above: Class 37s were never a common sight on the S&C; indeed, an entire pictorial book by an expert on the line, showing trains on the route from the start of 'dieselisation' in the 1960s up to and including the 1980s, does not contain a single photograph of an English Electric Type 3! Making a change from top-and-tail operations is this Crewe–Carlisle charter of 29 December 2003, featuring not merely double-headed '37s' but, more interestingly, a Loadhaul/EWS livery mix. Class 37/5s Nos 37 698 (with red side door!) and 37 668 are seen near Waitby. Neither locomotive could supply train heating, so on this winter's day a generator van was coupled next to the 'Syphons'. *Gavin Morrison*

Right: This photograph has all the ingredients that combine to produce a superb impression of a Settle & Carlisle train in the landscape: bright sunlight in the foreground, a dramatic sky, mysterious distant hills, dry stone walls and a colourful train all contribute to a classic image. Heading north near Waitby are Nos 37 411 *The Scottish Railway Preservation Society* and 37 408 *Loch Rannoch* with the 09.47 Leeds–Carlisle on 13 November 2003. The last day of '37'-hauled services over the line was 25 September 2004, and, by coincidence, the final train was powered by the two locomotives featured here. *Gavin Morrison*

Gloucester Routes

Left: An unrefurbished Class 37 in BR Rail blue passes through Chepstow station, on the main line between Severn Tunnel Junction and Gloucester. The train originated from Tintern Quarry, on the old Monmouth branch line, and has just crossed the bridge over the River Wye, which can be seen in the background (right). The station buildings demonstrate the contrast between the levels of comfort afforded the travelling public in the Victorian era and those expected today. *Author*

Below: In charge of just two wagons, No 37 004 passes through a wintry landscape south of Norton Junction, near Worcester, in November 1989. The train would leave the main line at Barnwood Junction, Gloucester, and run along the banks of the River Severn via Lydney on its way to South Wales. As No D6704, one of the earliest EE Type 3s delivered, in January 1961 to Stratford depot in East London, the locomotive (still based at Stratford) by now belonged to the Railfreight Distribution LNRA (Freightliner) pool. *Author*

Above: Between Standish Junction, south of Gloucester, and Swindon is a splendid section of line known locally as the Golden Valley. Included in the eastbound run is the long climb to Sapperton Tunnel, which involves crossing Frampton Mansell Viaduct, just visible in this photograph from May 1982. No 37 134 could be heard a considerable distance away as it growled up to Sapperton with a train of empty newspaper vans returning to Old Oak Common. *Author*

Below: Gloucester has long been associated with Class 37s, mainly at the head of freight trains. Standish Junction, south of the city, is where the one-time Midland route from Bristol, seen here in the foreground, is joined by the ex-GW route from Swindon and London. Descending from Stonehouse with more than 1,000 tonnes in tow is No 37 177 with train 4M31, the 17.45 FSX Swindon–Longbridge, containing car parts. The train was a dedicated service operated for British Leyland, later Austin Rover and now defunct. Gloucester remains an important junction, although rail traffic has diminished over recent decades. It once had a thriving locomotive depot, but this was later reduced in status to a mere stabling point. On the bright side, it was announced in 2005 that Cotswold Rail, no doubt attracted by rail access in all directions, would be using Gloucester Horton Road as its headquarters. *Author*

Above: One of the most interesting Class 37 experiments took place in the late 1980s, when six locomotives were selected to act as guinea pigs for rival 1,800hp diesel engines from Mirrlees and Ruston. Nos 37 905 and 37 906 (formerly 37 136 and 37 206) were each fitted with a GEC G564AZ alternator and a 12-cylinder Ruston RK270T engine. Immaculate in original Railfreight livery (without a red solebar stripe), No 37 906 stands in Gloucester Yard on 4 September 1987 with a train from South Wales. *Norman E. Preedy*

Below: The numbers, names and liveries of most Class 37s have changed so many times that a detailed analysis would be appropriate only in a book dedicated to the subject. By way of example, No 37 427 started life as No D6988 and became successively 6988 and 37 288 before adopting its final identity; before being named *Highland Enterprise* it was *Bont Y Bermo*, which name is now carried by No 37 402! It carried many liveries but was unique in being given Regional Railways colours with ScotRail lettering, in which form it is seen at Gloucester station on 10 October 1995. *Norman E. Preedy*

Cornwall

Right: Class 37s did not appear in the county of Cornwall until 1979, when the first examples arrived to replace Class 25s. Thereafter they had a stranglehold of the local china-clay trains for more than 20 years, until Class 66s began to infiltrate the ranks. From October 1996 freight operations were taken over by EWS, which adopted a colour scheme based on that of then owner Wisconsin Central. One of the earliest repaints noted in the area was No 37 521, seen in June 1997 rolling into Lostwithiel with a rake of CDA wagons loaded with china clay destined for the docks at Carne Point, Fowey. *Author*

Left: In days gone by the amount of freight traffic in West Cornwall was considerable. Outbound commodities included seasonal farm produce, flowers, post and parcels, milk, seaweed, beer and scrap, while in went oil, coal, fertiliser and general merchandise. Currently the only freight traffic west of Truro is a weekly train of fuel tankers for use by the railway at Ponsandane depot, near Penzance. In this delightful view of the 100ft-high, 798ft-long Angarrack Viaduct (an 1885 replacement of the original Brunel structure), a Transrail Class 37 heads seven four-wheel tankers on their weekly return run to Tavistock Junction. *Author*

Above: In the 1980s an experiment was conducted whereby a degree of management and operational autonomy was granted to railway operations in Cornwall, and the marketing name Cornish Railways was coined. There were similarities with the creation of operating sectors, which were to follow. One of St Blazey's Class 37s, No 37 207 *William Cookworthy*, had 'Cornish Railways' applied to its nose ends, together with a crest featuring both British Rail and Kernow flags. On a quite delightful 22 July 1986 'Cookers' emerges from the bridge at Stoneycross and approaches Treesmill with a down rake of empty clay hoods. *Author*

Below: A high-level photograph of a Class 37 at Golant was first published in the Ian Allan volume *Diesels in the Duchy* back in 1983, and no apologies are made for including further shots at this idyllic location. On a cracking afternoon in April 1990 No 37 671 *Tre Pol and Pen* in triple-grey Railfreight livery provides the power (and braking!) for a 32-wagon, 1,800-tonne load of china clay as it runs down from Lostwithiel along the banks of the River Fowey and crosses the causeway at Golant. The train is making for the docks at Carne Point, where the 'white gold' will be loaded onto waiting ships for export. *Author*

Above: Overlooking the steep climb to Treverrin Tunnel, between Lostwithiel and Par, finds a named Transrail Class 37, thought to be No 37 674 *Saint Blaise Church*, giving its all with a rake of empty CDA air-braked china-clay hoppers. The deciduous tree, crumbling outbuilding, horses and sheep provide atmosphere on a dull misty day. At this time a block of refurbished Class 37/5s, Nos 37 669-675, were allocated to Plymouth Laira's FTLL pool, primarily for china-clay duties, although light maintenance was carried out at St Blazey depot. *Author*

Left: Once sectorisation had taken place it was always satisfying to secure photographs of locomotives working trains from other than their specific sector or subsector. Such was the case in August 1994 when Railfreight triple-grey No 37 229, its decal of black diamonds on a yellow background denoting allocation to the Coal subsector, worked the 17.00 St Blazey–Exeter Riverside air-braked freight, comprising tank wagons containing china-clay slurry. The train is pictured passing Restormel, between Lostwithiel and Bodmin Parkway. *Author*

Above: This photograph, from June 1986, affords a late-afternoon high-level view of the Lostwithiel station area. An all-blue Class 37 is just starting the climb to Treverrin Tunnel — in places as steep as 1 in 57 — with a long haul of empty clay hoods. Of particular note is the huge number of wagons in the down sidings, which, given that there were only about 450 wagons in service at this time, represented a sizeable proportion of the total fleet. Also visible are some milk tankers, at the down bay platform once used by passenger trains to Fowey. *Author*

Left: Small boats in echelon at high tide provide foreground interest at Golant on the old Fowey branch. The line has an interesting history, having been opened as a broad-gauge line in 1869 but closed in 1879 due to competition in the clay-distribution industry, and because significant capital expenditure on the infrastructure was required. The GWR reopened the branch as a standard-gauge line in 1895. Passenger services ceased in January 1965. Without subsector decals, No 37 676 heads for Carne Point, just north of the town of Fowey, in July 1999, only a few months before the arrival in Cornwall of the first Class 66s. *Author*

Above: The first Railfreight-liveried Class 37s to arrive in Cornwall were refurbished machines that had had their generators replaced by alternators. In absolutely resplendent condition with red buffer-beam, No 37 696 arrives at Liskeard with a train of clay hoods in August 1986. The locomotive was fitted with dual brakes, so these old vacuum-braked wagons would have presented no problem; however, the hoods would be withdrawn *en masse* in February 1988, so this locomotive/wagon combination was to be seen for only a relatively short time. *Author*

Below: A picture summing up the Cornish china-clay scene of the mid-1980s, which in retrospect were halcyon days. On a simply superb summer's day in 1986, with clouds brushing the hills on the eastern side of the Fowey estuary, No 37 207 *William Cookworthy*, in full Cornish Railways regalia, passes the high tide at the hamlet of Golant with empty clay hoods for ECC's Rocks Works at Goonbarrow Junction, on the Newquay branch. It was a sad day when the Class 37s finally disappeared from daily rail operations west of the River Tamar. *Author*

Border Country

Left: Another line to have enjoyed a long association with Class 37 locomotives is the North & West route through the Border counties of England and Wales, sometimes referred to as the Welsh Marches. In the early-morning sunlight and looking very purposeful at the head of a Dee Marsh–Llanwern train of steel bars on 1 August 1991 are Class 37/5s Nos 37 503 *British Steel Sheldon* and 37 502 (formerly *British Steel Teesside*). With Shrewsbury Abbey as a backdrop the train is seen approaching Sutton Bridge Junction. *Author*

Left: The scenery along much of the North & West route is breathtaking, as exemplified in this view near Marshbrook in May 1992. With the Long Mynd, above Church Stretton, in the background No 37 250 of the FMYI (Railfreight Metals, Immingham) pool hauls 15 metal-laden wagons of varying vintages from Dee Marsh to South Wales. Since this photograph was taken changes to the structure of the steel industry and the emergence of the Corus company (itself soon to be taken over) have seen a decrease in the number of such trains. *Author*

Above: It is not often that a railway photographer happens to be in the right place at the right time and with the right lens (in this case a 300mm Nikkor) on the camera. However, on 15 July 1988 the author captured an exhaust explosion erupting from No 37 427 *Bont Y Bermo* departing Shrewsbury with the 10.00 Manchester Piccadilly–Cardiff. The precise location is Sutton Bridge Junction, where the Cambrian line (visible on the left) diverges. At this time a handful of passenger trains on the route were locomotive-hauled, due to the non-availability of Class 155 DMUs. The name *Bont Y Bermo* ('Barmouth Bridge') would later be transferred to No 37 402. *Author*

Right: Another example of the importance of the North & West route to the steel industry is demonstrated by this heavy train of steel coil bound for the British Steel Corporation works at Shotton, near Dee Marsh, on 31 July 1991. The train had been 'looped' at Sutton Bridge Junction to allow a faster passenger train to pass; note that the starting signal for the passing-loop is of the upper-quadrant variety whereas the main-line home signal is of the lower-quadrant type. No 37 040, leading, was an unrefurbished example, but No 37 520 was a refurbished '37/5'; both locomotives were allocated to far-off Motherwell. *Author*

Left: Until 31 July 1961 Woofferton was the junction station for trains to Tenbury Wells, but nowadays it is merely the location of an intermediate block post between Hereford and Shrewsbury. Passing the elderly signalbox and a fine array of signals is Class 37/9 No 37 904 heading a scrap-metal train for South Wales on 4 May 1988. Along with Nos 37 901-903 this locomotive emerged from refurbishment in 1986/7 fitted with a Mirrlees MB275T eight-cylinder 1,800hp engine, which power unit was being considered for the proposed new Class 38 design. The Class 38 was subsequently abandoned, but these locomotives nevertheless served as useful testbeds for an engine that would be employed in more powerful (3,100hp) form in the Class 60s. All the '37/9s' were allocated to a special Metals-subsector pool based on Cardiff Canton. *Author*

Right: Among the most colourful trains to traverse the North & West route in the 1980s was the Cawoods anthracite workings to/from Abercwmboi, on the Aberdare branch in South Wales. Heading a long rake of air-braked orange and white empties past the site of Dorrington station on 4 May 1988 is heavyweight Class 37/7 No 37 897 of the FECA (Railfreight Power Station Coal) pool, based at Cardiff Canton. At this time it was refreshing to have an alternative to all-blue locomotives, but nowadays one would be pleased to see any locomotive in the viewfinder! *Author*

Left: In May 1988 it was something of a scoop to capture on film Nos 37 905 and 37 906, the two 1,800hp GEC-Ruston-engined Class 37/9s. Converted from Nos 37 136 and 37 206 respectively, they were the only '37/9s' fitted with slow-speed control. On a delightful evening No 37 905 *Vulcan Enterprise* is seen testing both engine and traction motors with a 1,300-tonne load of steel coil passing Dorrington signalbox with a Shotton/Dee Marsh–Llanwern working. *Author*

Scottish Lowlands

Above: As used here 'Lowlands' is a very loose description, used to differentiate the majority of Scotland from the West Highlands and the Far North. Consequently only a small (but hopefully representative) sample of Class 37 workings can be illustrated in the space available. A wide range of Class 37-hauled trains have performed all over Scotland, ranging from heavy coal trains working between Hunterstone and Ravenscraig near Motherwell, to light freights trundling along the Menstrie branch, near Stirling. Deep in Ayrshire, at Chalmerston on the Waterside branch from Dalrymple Junction, Coal subsector Nos 37 693 *Sir William Arrol* and 37 375 are loaded at the opencast coal-mining site on 25 September 1992. *Gavin Morrison*

Right: Situated between Scotland's largest city, Glasgow, and its capital, Edinburgh, is Cumbernauld, which has grown hugely since it gained 'new town' status in the 1960s. During a visit back in April 1987 the photographer was so surprised at the sound and speed of this Grangetown–Mossend tanker train that he was unable to write down the numbers! Both locomotives have wrap-round yellow cab ends, the first (believed to be No 37 191), in full 'large logo' livery bearing a white West Highland terrier motif, the second a Highland Rail stag. *Author*

Above: As was the case on the Liverpool Street–Cambridge line, locomotive-hauled services between the Rivers Tay and Forth were retained well into the 1980s. The coaches used thereon were steam-heated, so it was necessary to retain compatible motive power. Many Class 37s still had their Clayton RO 2500/3 boilers, which had a steaming capacity of 2,000lb/hr. Here steam can be seen escaping from the train-heating pipe and from beneath the rear bogie of No 37 191, waiting to depart from the bay platform at Dundee with the 10.28 service to Edinburgh Waverley. The photograph was taken on 19 October 1984, by which date the semaphore signals had only weeks to live. *Author*

Left: Class 37s were also active on the east coast of Scotland at the head of passenger and freight trains, although the latter predominated. Unusual motive power for 1S99, an additional Scarborough–Glasgow summer-holiday train, on 29 July 1978 was Thornaby's No 37 161. The train is seen in glorious surroundings at Cockburnspath, between Berwick-on-Tweed and Dunbar. Thornaby depot was the recipient of a large part of the second batch of EE Type 3s to be built when, in late 1962, it gained Nos D6755-78. *Peter J. Robinson*

If there was ever a monument to Scottish railway engineering it must surely be the massive Forth Bridge. Designed by Sir John Fowler and Benjamin Baker, employing the balanced-cantilever principle, it was the world's first major steel bridge, started in 1883 and completed in 1890. Sadly 57 men lost their lives during its construction. Every statistic relating to it is mind-boggling. It is 1½ miles long, has a girder span of 1,710ft, contains 54,000 tons of steel and cost £3.2 million (equivalent to £235 million today) to build. A significant £40 million refurbishment took place in 1998. In this view, recorded on 20 October 1984, No 37 201 darkens the sky as it blasts away from the bridge towards Dalmeny station with a southbound freight. *Author*

Steel Blue

Above: Following the creation in the mid-1980s of various freight sectors, including Railfreight, a number of different liveries eventually emerged, each relating to the industry served. One of the more striking examples was the sky-blue 'large logo' scheme adopted by British Steel. The livery was unique to Class 37/5 No 37 501 *Teesside Steelmaster* and had a short life, being applied in February 1987 and superseded (by Railfreight's new triple-grey scheme) in August 1989. This view at Clay Cross Junction, south of Chesterfield, features the locomotive double-heading No 37 502 *British Steel Teesside* (in the original Railfreight livery but with red solebar stripe) on a train making for the Derby line on 11 November 1988. Note the British Steel logo just ahead of the driver's door. *Gavin Morrison*

Left: The same pair of locomotives seen again pulling together in multiple, this time at Gloucester on 26 April 1988. Refurbished Class 37/5s Nos 37 501 and 37 502 leave the city with train 6E47 from Cardiff (Tidal Sidings) to Tees Yard. The '37s' could work in multiple with up to two other members of the class or with other locomotives fitted with 'blue star' electro-pneumatic coupling equipment. *Norman E. Preedy*

SERCo in Sussex

Right: Following the mass withdrawal of EWS Class 37s and the abandonment of some previously 'Syphon'-hauled freight services, appearances on the erstwhile Central Division of the Southern Region became very infrequent. It was therefore refreshing during 2006 when DRS won the contract to haul SERCo test/track-recording trains in the area. Beautifully illuminated by the early-evening sun (at 19.01) on 3 July 2006, No 37 611 blasts through Worthing at the head of the formation, with sister locomotive No 37 609 bringing up the rear. The train would travel as far as Preston Park before returning west. *Author*

Below: It's nearly 8pm at Goring-by-Sea, West Sussex, on 3 July 2006 as the SERCo test train heads west, now with No 37 609 leading and No 37 611 at the rear. Note the red buffer-beam, evidence of silver buffers and the neat modern light clusters. SERCo provides rail-testing services, including the investigation and analysis of track and vehicle-related problems. In December 2002 SERCo Railtest Ltd reached agreement with Network Rail Infrastructure Ltd for track access until March 2009. *Author*

Down to Weymouth

Left: The old Great Western Railway route from Castle Cary to Weymouth is very rural and, outside the towns of Yeovil and Dorchester, is sparsely populated. Long sections of the line were singled many years ago as an economy measure, which reflected the relatively infrequent train service. Here, in June 1993, No 37 408 *Loch Rannoch* arrives at the double-faced up platform at Yeovil Pen Mill with a train for Bristol Temple Meads. Holiday trains such as this were known colloquially as 'bucket-and-spade specials'. Yeovil Pen Mill remains an oasis of semaphore signalling. *Author*

Left: For many years, in the summer season, Class 37s have worked down to Weymouth from Bristol on the former Great Western route via Yeovil. Just about every year for the last couple of decades has been proclaimed as 'the last year of operation', only for these venerable machines to appear on the line again the following year. No 37 197, in yellow and grey Civil Engineer's livery, was photographed approaching Yeovil Pen Mill station *en route* to Bristol in August 1992. A couple of golfers pause to observe the well-filled train, which has just passed the lower-quadrant home signal. The line on the right is the freight-only spur from Yeovil Junction, on the Salisbury–Exeter line. *Author*

Left: South of Yeovil are a number of former halts, including Thornford, Yetminster and Chetnole. Yetminster was a great place to photograph the summer-only Class 37s, because once the 'Syphon'/'Growler'/'Tractor' had rushed by to the Dorset coast it was a pleasure to wander into the village, where there was a delightful hostelry! However, on this day the visit was by road, and in view of the time and investment involved in travelling to the area, the train was worth a chase in an attempt to secure a second photograph! Passing a 'rationalised' Yetminster in August 1993 is No 37 425 *Sir William McAlpine / Concrete Bob* with a train for Weymouth. *Author*

Right: Without endangering life or limb the photographer succeeded in capturing the train again, this time on Southern Region electrified metals south of Dorchester, exiting Bincombe Tunnel and descending to the seaside terminus of Weymouth. Although the Class 37/4s were ETH-fitted and might therefore be regarded as passenger locomotives, many carried freight livery and were used as multi-purpose machines, among them No 37 425, which at this time carried Trainload Construction livery. In April 2005 this locomotive was outshopped by Toton TMD in a 'heritage' livery of 'large logo' blue. *Author*

Below: Over the years summer timetables have varied, the Class 37s working variously a single Bristol–Weymouth round-trip, two round-trips or one full round-trip with a fill-in 'short' from Weymouth to Westbury and return. A delightful survivor of GWR days is the overall roof at Frome station. While expresses between Paddington and the West Country bypass the Somerset market town by means of an avoiding line, it is served by the majority of Weymouth-line trains. Class 37/4 No 37 412 *Driver John Elliott*, in Transrail livery, is seen departing with a train from Bristol in July 1995. *Author*

Transrail

Left: The Railfreight subsectors survived until 1994, when, in preparation for privatisation, there was a restructuring whereby three operating companies were formed: Transrail, Loadhaul and Mainline. The Transrail organisation was formed, in broad terms, to run freight services on the western side of the UK. Part of its operations included china-clay trains in Cornwall and Devon. In this view beside the River Fowey, recorded from the hamlet of Golant in June 1996, the main points of interest are Transrail Class 37 No 37 674 *Saint Blaise Church* and the Fisherman's Arms pub on the left. *Author*

Left: Transrail saved itself the expense of repainting by retaining the existing Railfreight livery, to which was added a large white 'T' on a dark blue background surrounded by a red circle, the whole being underlined with two bold red lines; alongside was the word 'transrail' in white capital letters. The livery is seen on No 37 668 at Lostwithiel in June 1996. Locomotives in 'Dutch' livery (and one in BR blue) also received the 'big T' without repainting. *Author*

Left: Transrail was launched in Cornwall on 9 October 1994, but the company lasted only a further two years, because on 21 October 1996 the Trainload Freight businesses were sold to the Wisconsin Central Corporation of the USA, which duly merged them to form the English, Welsh & Scottish Railway (EWS). EWS adopted the parent company's house colours of deep red and gold, but it was some time before the entire fleet could be repainted, and as far as the Class 37s were concerned this was an objective never fully achieved. In March 1997 EWS Class 37 No 37 670 *St. Blazey T&RS Depot*, still in Transrail livery, heads into the setting sun on the down main line at Lostwithiel. *Author*

Above: It would be impossible to contrive a scene to rival this stunning view of a train in the picturesque British landscape. Seen from across Claverton Weir (between Bath and Trowbridge on the delightful River Avon) in early-morning light on a perfect spring day, No 37 407 *Blackpool Tower* heads the 07.40 Westbury–Bath empty coaching stock on 2 May 1994. From Bath Spa the train would form a commuter service to Bristol Temple Meads before returning south as the 09.00 Bristol–Weymouth. *Rail Photoprints*

Below: Another attractive Somerset scene just east of Somerton features an interesting combination of Transrail locomotives heading an engineers' spoil train from Exeter Riverside to Westbury. The work-stained pair — Class 37/7 No 37 887 in Transrail livery (adapted from the later Railfreight scheme) and unrefurbished No 37 043 in Departmental 'Dutch' livery with 'T' transfers — are seen negotiating the curves of the GW main line on 15 March 1999. Freight trains on this stretch of line have been infrequent in recent years, with sometimes only weekly oil trains and irregular aggregate and ballast workings operating. *Rail Photoprints*

Triple Headers

Above: It is normally the railways of North America that routinely indulge in multiple-heading (although even there the number of locomotives involved has reduced as super-powerful third-generation motive power has come on stream). However, in the UK the sight of three locomotives at the head of a train is always bound to get shutters firing. Rolling through rural East Anglia at Thurston, between Stowmarket and Bury St Edmunds, is the diverted 07.54 Stratford–Parkeston Quay Freightliner of 19 January 1991. Behind Class 37/7s Nos 37 709 and 37 890 can be seen 5,000hp 25kV Class 90 electric No 90 047, which was obviously 'dead in train'. *Brian Morrison*

Below: Without doubt the most famous regular triple-heading of Class 37s was on the heavy Port Talbot–Llanwern iron-ore trains in the 1970s. A total of 5,250hp (gross) was thus available before the arrival in South Wales of the Class 56s, following which such trains were hauled by these 3,250hp locomotives operating in pairs. Here Nos 37 184, 37 304 and 37 299, operating in multiple with a single traincrew, enter the vast Llanwern complex on 19 December 1979. *Author*

Above: This quite remarkable sight is barely believable, but it was recorded long before the era of digital photography, with its ample scope for manipulating images! Leaving an exhaust trail over Bristol Temple Meads station on Sunday 20 June 1993, a trio of 'Dutch'-liveried Departmental (or 'Infrastructure') locomotives — Nos 37 092, 37 158 and 37 197 — head a BR staff special from Paddington to Paignton. *Gavin Morrison*

Below: An impressive combination at Bell Busk, between Skipton and Hellifield, on 27 December 1991 as a Regional Railways special from Leeds to Carlisle is triple-headed by Departmental Class 37s Nos 37 071 and 37 083 from the Civil Engineer's DCEA (Eastern) pool, based at Immingham, and Rail Express Systems (Postal Sector) Class 47/4 No 47 479 *Track 29* in Post Office red and dark grey. The train has a small 'Anglia Boys' headboard. *Gavin Morrison*

Left: An exceptionally rare sight at Blackpool clay driers at Burngullow in Cornwall on 21 April 1993 as a trio of Class 37s head a rake of empty CDA china-clay wagons. Posing for the camera are Nos 37 673, 37 674 and 37 671 *Tre Pol and Pen*, all in the standard tri-tone-grey Railfreight livery that first appeared in the county in the latter part of 1988. In the same year English China Clays spent £2 million modernising this site to enable it to handle new loads of china-clay slurry. ECC was later taken over by French company Imerys. *Author*

Below left: Although the subject is too large to be covered comprehensively in this volume, the preservation of Class 37s is already well underway. By the end of 2006 more than 40 examples had been acquired for this purpose, while a number of others were still working for main-line companies. Taking part in the Mid-Hants Railway's 'Trainspotters Ball 3' event of 28 April 2002, Nos 37 065 in Mainline blue, 37 308 in standard BR blue and 37 190 in the attractive 'large logo' scheme arrive at Medstead & Four Marks station with the 16.55 from Alresford to Alton. *P. G. Barnes*

Below: Redundant Class 37s have been exported to both France and Spain to help with construction and infrastructure projects. By August 1999 a total of 20 EWS locomotives were based at the LGV Mediterranée Construction base at Eurre in France, and more were to follow. Here Nos 37 100 in Transrail triple-grey, 37 196 in 'Dutch' livery and an unidentified example (believed to be No 37 274) in Mainline blue pass Donzère with train 414E from Mondragon to Eurre on 14 April 2000. In 2001 an initial 14 EWS Class 37s were sent to Spain for use on the construction of a new high-speed line between Barcelona and Madrid, painted in the two-tone-blue livery of operator GIF. *Colin J. Marsden*

Silver Bullet

Right: An exciting new traffic source commenced during 1989 with the introduction of a flow of china-clay slurry from Burngullow in Cornwall to Irvine in Scotland. Conveyed in shiny new aluminium tankers, each with a gross (loaded) weight of 90 tonnes, the slurry would be used in the manufacture of paper by the Caledonian Paper Co. Frequency has varied over the years, peaking with a thrice-weekly round-trip operation. Seen through a powerful 300mm Nikkor lens, a 900-tonne 'Silver Bullet' blasts across Bolitho Viaduct in September 1994 behind Class 37/4 No 37 412 and '37/5' No 37 671 *Tre Pol and Pen*. The semaphore signal is Liskeard's outer home, the first manual signal encountered on a journey from Paddington. *Author*

Below: The 'Silver Bullet' is routed via Bristol, the North & West route and the West Coast main line, giving rise to the interesting sight of china clay being transported through rural Shropshire. Making a change from the usual Railfreight livery are a pair of Class 37/4s in unbranded InterCity livery (known as BR 'main line' livery — not to be confused with the later Mainline blue), both with Scottish-flavoured names! Nos 37 417 *Highland Region* and 37 420 *The Scottish Hosteller* pass Craven Arms on their way to Scotland in April 1992. Pairs of Class 37s were replaced on these workings in July 1995 by single Class 60s. *Author*

Specials

Left: Over the past four and a half decades Class 37s have always been in demand to head railway enthusiasts' special trains. Many of the freight examples were difficult for haulage fans to travel behind, and operators had little trouble selling seats when such motive power was assured. In this November 1979 photograph the Railway Pictorial Publications Railtours (RPPR) 'Stoneliner' tour (organised by the author) from Paddington arrives at Radstock — then the end of the freight-only branch from Frome — behind grubby Nos 37 232 and 37 204. *Author*

Left: Accident victims aside, withdrawals commenced only in the early 1990s, by which time many locomotives were already over 30 years of age. By then the preservation movement, with aspirations of securing members of the class, was well established, and some organisations operated special trains for supporters in order to raise funds. In April 1991 the Growler Group ran its 'Solent Growler' tour to the Southampton area, hauled by a pair of unrefurbished Railfreight machines — Nos 37 272 (ex 37 304) in triple-grey with red and yellow (Distribution) decals and 37 032 in the original grey. The special is seen leaving Eastleigh, with scores of heads leaning from the windows of the Mk 1 rolling stock. *Author*

Left: On 21 May 1995 the Growler Group was still active in the railtour business, but this time it was the 'Medway Growler' tour that was photographed, in pouring rain at Reigate, Surrey, on the line from Guildford to Redhill. The power on this occasion was provided by a miniature-snowplough-fitted Regional Railways-liveried Class 37/4, No 37 421 *The Kingsman*. The pioneer EE Type 3, No D6700, was donated by EWS to the National Railway Museum in October 2000, and by early 2007 the '37s' in preservation numbered 40 examples. *Author*

A truly exceptional structure is Lockwood Viaduct, south of Huddersfield on the line to Penistone and Barnsley, which was formerly a through route to Sheffield. Crossing the impressive 32 arches on Saturday 13 October 1979 is RPPR's 'Hull Hornet', which toured a number of northern railway 'hotspots', with 10 loaded Mk 1 coaches hauled by a pair of 'Growlers' in the shape of Nos 37 252 and 37 221. On this bleak autumn day these dual-braked Immingham freight locomotives could provide no train heating – a hardship gladly endured by the participants! *Gavin Morrison*

Western Main

Left: A matching pair of Departmental locomotives on an engineering train on the WR main line west of Reading. 'Dutch'-liveried Nos 37 012 and 37 264 head through Moreton Cutting, east of Didcot, with a long mixed train of track components and ballast in May 1993. Both locomotives were then based at Cardiff and allocated to the DCWA pool. *Author*

Left: Traditionally, train classifications (from 1 to 9) were based on a number of factors, including the type of rolling stock in the consist and the braking ability of the formation, but the 'bottom line' is the maximum permitted speed of the train. This train will be in the slowest Class 9 category and limited to 45mph. Passing the attractive setting of Ruscombe, east of Twyford, on the up slow line at 14.00 on 8 May 1992 is No 37 097 with a delightful ragbag of Departmental vehicles. *Author*

Right: Paths for slow-moving trains on the WR main line during daylight hours are hard to find, but one such was found on 18 April 1992 for the 16.15 from West Ruislip to Didcot (and ultimately Horbury, in Yorkshire). The train consists of London Transport Underground 'tube' stock heading for heavy maintenance or refurbishment at the Bombardier works near Wakefield. At each end of the formation is a barrier vehicle to permit compatible coupling. Running well ahead of its booked time, the train is seen passing Lower Basildon, in the Thames Valley, behind Railfreight Distribution-liveried No 37 063. *P. G. Barnes*

Below Right: Over the years domestic coal trains from South Wales to the Southern Region gradually reduced in length as users switched to other energy sources. Three such workings that regularly used the Western Region main line were the 6V04 Redhill–Didcot (originating from Hove, Sussex), 6V32 Chessington South–Didcot and 6V38 Temple Mills–Didcot. All tended to be Class 37-hauled. On 5 May 1990 Railfreight Coal No 37 213 is seen approaching Taplow with a train from Hove comprising five empty red HEA wagons. Sadly the Chessington service ended in 1988, and the Hove would soon follow suit. *Author*

Below: Sometimes coal empties from more than one originating point could be combined, but on this occasion in July 1989 returning empties from the Blue Circle cement works at Westbury were sufficient in number to form a single block load. Having travelled via the 'Berks & Hants' route through Reading West to reach Didcot, No 37 167 of Cardiff Canton's FQLC Coal Distribution pool approaches Cholsey & Moulsford on the down slow line with 36 HEA hoppers. *Author*

Land of St David

Above: Only by studying the railway gazetteer does one begin to realise how far the lines of West Wales are from the major industrial centres of South Wales. For example, Fishguard Harbour is more than 110 miles from Cardiff, and with a lower frequency of trains the area is somewhat neglected by railway photographers. In this scene from the past, dating back to 10 August 1979, No 37 182 shunts the yard at Haverfordwest on the Milford Haven branch, with brake vans at either end of this local coal train. Note also the box vans in the background. *Les Bertram*

Left: Over the years there have always been railway connections with ferry services across the Irish Sea between Fishguard Harbour and Rosslare. Connecting train services are infrequent, and although most run to Swansea there have also been through express trains to Paddington. One such boat-train express storms through Clunderwen, between Clarbeston Road and Whitland, in August 1983 behind No 37 301. The platforms here are staggered, and on the up side a small shelter has replaced a fine station building. *Author*

At the end of a long summer's day in 1983, a Nikon FM2 camera with a 35mm f2 Nikkor semi-wide-angle lens was used to record, from the fine old goods shed at Llanelli, No 37 266 departing for Swansea with a train from Fishguard Harbour. The use of this freight locomotive on a passenger train was portentous, because it was later converted to Class 37/4 No 37 422. In May 1993 it was given the name *Robert F. Fairlie — Locomotive Engineer 1831-1885*, but this was later superseded by its current name of *Cardiff Canton. Author*

The association of Class 37s with the North East of England dates back to the turn of 1962/3, when Nos D6784-95 were allocated to Gateshead MPD, following on from examples already allocated to Hull Dairycoates, Darnall (Sheffield) and Thornaby-on-Tees. Eventually Gateshead depot closed, and certain facilities were removed to Tyne Yard, seen here. In this 30 August 1994 view Class 37/5 No 37 697 is at the head of a mineral train, while on the right are successors in the shape of Type 5s Nos 56 107 and 60 046 *William Wilberforce. Brian Morrison*

Above: After more than 100 English Electric Type 3 locomotives had been constructed it was decided that the hinged double doors on the cab ends were superfluous. From No D6819 (later 37 283 and then 37 895) locomotives were built without these doors and with a single, central one-piece headcode panel on each nose end. In original green livery but with full yellow ends, No D6894 heads a southbound Class 8 coal train across the River Wear at Sunderland on 29 August 1967. *Brian Stephenson*

Below: The stereotypical infrastructure of a northern town is illustrated in this view of factories and terraced houses in the city of Durham. Crossing the impressive Durham Viaduct in grubby workaday condition is split-headcode Class 37 No 37 061 with a mixed freight for Tyneside on 13 May 1980. This locomotive was allocated to Gateshead and spent much of its life in the North East. At this time it was fitted with vacuum brakes only and was thus restricted to hauling old-fashioned goods wagons, as here. *Author*

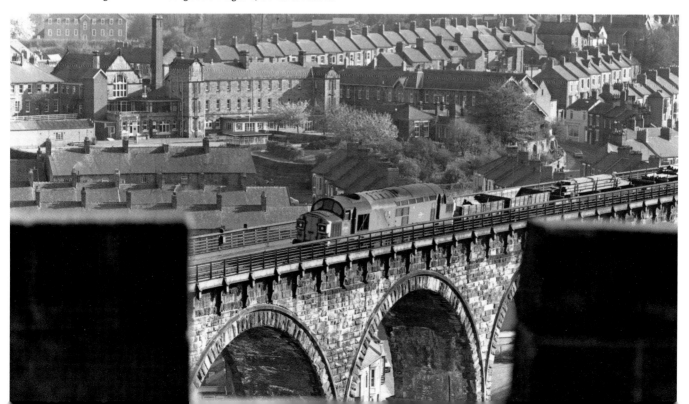

Above: This remarkable view of Thornaby's No 37 067, bringing together rail, road and river at a single location, was recorded on 30 June 1977 to the west of Bishop Auckland, on the erstwhile North Eastern Railway's Wearhead branch. The 'Syphon' is heading empty 'Presflo' wagons to Eastgate for loading and is seen crossing the River Wear, while threading the bridge supports is the Witton Park–High Grange road. *Rodney Wildsmith*

Left: From a railway photographer's standpoint there can be equal æsthetic appeal in a heavy-industrial scene and a pleasant rural landscape. Firmly in the former category is this atmospheric panoramic view to the east of Middlesbrough. No 37 173 threads the vast Lackenby steelworks with an oil train that originated at Teesport on the south bank of the River Tees on 10 March 1977. Predictably, the locomotive was allocated to nearby Thornaby depot, and by this time it had been fitted with dual brakes. *Peter J. Robinson*

Right: Another view of Teesside's heavy industry, which over the years has generated large volumes of freight traffic. Passing under conveyors of various types and at a variety of angles at Grangetown, between Middlesbrough and Redcar, on 7 October 1975 is Gateshead's No 37 216. The Class 6 oil train, comprising large bogie tankers, is destined for Jarrow, on the River Tyne. *Ken Fleming*

Right: Presenting a sorry sight in faded original Railfreight livery is No 37 196. Just three years earlier, carrying the name *Tre Pol and Pen*, this locomotive had been the pride of Cornwall, but by the time it was photographed in the North East, on 11 March 1989, only the scars left by the plates remained. In the meantime it had been moved around the UK, including a spell at Inverness. It is seen at Penshaw North, heading up the Leamside Line — a diversionary route that keeps slow-moving freights off the East Coast main line — with a mixed freight destined for the sidings at Ferryhill, Co Durham. *Ian S. Carr*

Right: An amusing — not to say bizarre — episode in the Class 37 story occurred during 1985 when No 37 093 (later No 37 509) was repainted in 'Police' livery for use in a television commercial, in which it chased, caught up with and arrested a speeding HST IC125 unit on the adjacent track. Filming took place between Haltwhistle and Haydon Bridge on the Newcastle–Carlisle line. The locomotive, in white with red and orange bands, is seen at Haltwhistle on 23 July. *Ian S. Carr*

Fenland Junction

Left: Until the downturn of the last decade or two the town of March, in Cambridgeshire, and the nearby Whitemoor marshalling yard constituted a major railway centre. The multiple sidings in the March/Whitemoor area were used for marshalling freights, for traincrew and locomotive changes and for storage, while lines once radiated to Ely, Spalding, Wisbech, Peterborough and St Ives. In this February 1985 view No 37 123 hauls a couple of vans into March station from Whitemoor. *Author*

Below: March was a mecca for Class 37 fans, although large numbers of Class 31s, 45s and 47s could also be seen in the area during the 1980s. Seen passing the attractive station at 15.44 on 6 September 1986 is No 37 045, heading an engineers' track-laying train towards Ely. This locomotive was one of a number of Class 37s to have its fuel capacity increased to 1,689 gallons (from the original 830 gallons), an additional tank being located in the space once occupied by the water tank for the train-heating boiler. *Author*

Above: With hundreds of four-wheeled goods wagons occupying the sidings in the background, green-liveried No D6723 passes the lofty March East Junction signalbox and enters the station with a Class 7 train of empties in September 1968. Interestingly, the locomotive is propelling a brake tender of a type regularly seen on unfitted freights; the eight-wheeled tender was full of ballast, the weight adding considerably to the available braking capability of the locomotive and guard's van. Brake tenders gradually disappeared as more and more freight workings became at first partially braked and then fully fitted. *Author*

Below: A view typifying the flat Fenland 'produce and big sky' scenery in east Cambridgeshire and north Suffolk. Having left March and Ely far behind, No 37 034 traverses the single line near Soham with the four-vehicle 19.20SX air-braked freight from Mossend to Parkeston on 3 August 1985. *John C. Baker*

South Western

Above: None of the three divisions of the erstwhile Southern Region of BR were normally associated with Class 37s on a daily basis, but over the years members of the class were regular intruders. One of the highlights on the South Western Division in 1989 came on 7 July, when the normally Class 33-hauled 07.10 Whatley Quarry–Woking ballast train was double-headed by No 37 072 and SR Class 33/1 No 33 102. Working in multiple, made possible by a common 'blue star' coupling code, the pair are seen entering Salisbury station with a 1,100-tonne load of ballast-filled 'Seacows' in tow. *Author*

Below: A regular Class 37 turn on the South Western was the 6O64 oil train from Ripple Lane to Micheldever, Hampshire, where Elf and Amoco oil terminals and storage tanks were located on the down side of the station. Having propelled its train of by now empty bogie tankers out of the sidings, refurbished heavyweight Class 37/7 No 37 705 runs through Micheldever station on the up main in April 1989 at the start of the return journey to south Essex. *Author*

The small Foster Yeoman stone terminal at Botley straddles the trackbed of the old LSWR Bishop's Waltham branch line, which closed to passengers way back in 1932 and to goods in 1965. The two young lady passengers waiting for a train to Eastleigh seem disinterested as Nos 37 272 and 37 271, having arrived from Merehead via Westbury, unload their rake of 50-tonne four-wheeled Yeoman stone wagons on 5 March 1983. The signalbox had closed the previous year, when the control panel at Eastleigh assumed responsibility for all signalling in the area. *Author*

'37' Bugle Call

Above: Although Class 37s regularly worked to ECC's Rocks Works at Goonbarrow Junction on the Newquay branch they rarely strayed beyond; moreover trains seldom fail (at least in front of the camera), so securing not one but two photographs of the class at Bugle, both assisting failures, produced a sense of achievement. In the first such instance, on 4 October 1991, 'Bubble car' No 55006 had failed at Newquay (from where its passengers were taken on to Par by bus), and No 37 673 was despatched along the single line to retrieve the single-car DMU and haul it to St Blazey for repair. The colourful formation is seen approaching Bugle, with the abandoned Carbis Wharf branch on the left. *Author*

Below: On an appalling summer's day in August 1992 one of the power cars of a down InterCity 125 failed, and, with the formidable 1-in-37 climb to Luxulyan in prospect, the crew summoned assistance, which materialised in the form of two of St Blazey's Class 37s. Both sporting nameplates, Nos 37 675 (*William Cookworthy*) and 37 413 (less appropriately *Loch Eil Outward Bound*) haul HST power car No 43052 and the rest of the train away from Bugle and towards the Atlantic coast at Newquay. Note that in the intervening 10 months the Carbis Wharf branch featured in the previous illustration had been lifted. *Author*

Mainline

Above: One of the three Trainload Freight companies created in 1994 from the division of Railfreight was Mainline Freight, which assumed responsibility for freight operations in the South and East. The chosen livery was mid-blue with silver logo and lettering, displayed here by No 37 203 heading the Knowsley–Immingham freight (due off Healey Mills at 15.50) past Horbury on 2 April 2003. The company ceased to exist with the formation of EWS in 1996. *Gavin Morrison*

Right: This pair of Mainline-liveried Class 37s had obviously been working for some time without a clean. Accelerating away from Lostwithiel in June 1998 with a modest 240-tonne load in the shape of three 'Polybulk' wagons loaded with china clay, are this dirty duo headed by Nos 37 055, sporting a silver-and-red *RAIL* nameplate, and 37 274. The train is the late-afternoon air-braked freight from St Blazey to Exeter Riverside. The old dairy that once contributed rail traffic and supplied the capital with milk is on the right. *Author*

Somerset Stone

Left: For many years, especially after all the Western Region's diesel-hydraulics were withdrawn, Class 37s were regular performers in the Westbury area, hauling stone trains from Merehead and Whatley quarries. The demand for heavier and heavier trains called for pairs of Class 37s to be used in place of single Class 47s that had a lower power output and lacked sanding equipment. Seen passing the delightful Clink Road signalbox (long since demolished) in May 1982 are Nos 37 304 and 37 301 with empty stone hoppers for Merehead. *Author*

Below: The Class 37s disappeared from the stone-train circuit in favour of the new Class 56s, but the latter proved unreliable, and the 'Syphons' reappeared pending the arrival of the General Motors Class 59s in 1985. However, even after that date, the Type 3s could still be found on ARC trains, because the first Class 59s were privately owned by Foster Yeoman. Heading a heavy stone train of air-braked bogie wagons and four-wheelers from Whatley Quarry towards Fairwood Junction, Westbury on 9 October 1986, are Railfreight-liveried Nos 37 501 and 37 180 *County of Dyfed*. *Author*

It could be argued that the early 1980s were the halcyon days for pairs of Class 37s on stone trains working out of the Somerset quarries. Their high availability based on good reliability found favour, and, with the equivalent of Type 5 power output, pairs of Type 3s were the best option at that time. Avoiding the loop that serves the town of Frome, Nos 37 286 and 37 232 take the main-line cut-off between Blatchbridge Junction and Clink Road Junction on 21 March 1983 with an ex-Merehead working for the Foster Yeoman company. *Author*

Loadhaul

Above: The third of three 'shadow' freight companies created from Railfreight in 1994 was Loadhaul, encompassing freight activity in the North East. The livery adopted was arguably the most distinctive of the trio, featuring black, orange and yellow paintwork with large 'Loadhaul' branding on the bodysides. As ever with corporate liveries, there were a number of minor variations too tedious to detail here. In this crisp study No 37 698 passes Mirfield Shed bridge (and a westbound coal train) with a Knowsley–Immingham freight on 2 August 2004. *Gavin Morrison*

Left: Another view of No 37 698 in Loadhaul livery, working in that company's designated area but again very much in the era of EWS, which had simply not got round to repainting the locomotive in its colour scheme. Having left the large Healey Mills Yard, between Wakefield and Mirfield, it is seen heading east with a lengthy freight on 26 March 2003. Once allocated to Cardiff's Coal subsector, the locomotive was subsequently converted for use on Sandite workings.
Gavin Morrison

Right: In this beautifully lit photograph, taken on 10 March 1999, No 37 513 is working special train 8X09, the 20.45 Didcot–Horbury, comprising LUT 'tube' stock. Regular journeys are made between West Ruislip in Middlesex and Horbury in West Yorkshire, where such stock is refurbished at the Procor/Bombardier works. At each end of the rake of diminutive standard-gauge stock is a barrier vehicle, necessitated by the incompatibility of coupling systems. The train is seen in Horbury Cutting near the end of its journey. *Gavin Morrison*

Below: Middle Hill Tunnel, near Box, Wiltshire, was the unusual setting for Loadhaul-liveried No 37 516 on 9 February 1999. This impressive view of the Bristol Barrow Road portion of the 11.11 Calvert–Bath/Bristol 'Binliner' service would not have been possible had the booked Class 66 not failed; according to the photographer the black, orange and yellow replacement (albeit lacking Loadhaul branding) was 'most welcome'! The pale-blue containers are used to transport household and industrial waste to the disposal tip at Calvert, this being the empty return working. *Rail Photoprints*

Capital Power

Left: Although Liverpool Street station in Central London and Stratford depot to the east were among the first ports of call for the EE Type 3s in 1960/1 (and would remain Class 37 haunts until the 1980s), elsewhere around the capital they have been less numerous. Providing an unusual sight near St John's station, Lewisham, on 15 January 1995, Petroleum-subsector-liveried No 37 220 heads for London Bridge, where it will run round its ballast train before continuing to an engineering possession at Plumstead, east of Woolwich. *Brian Morrison*

Left: Kensington Olympia in West London is one of those locations where almost any type of train can turn up, and it produces plenty of surprises. In addition to local passenger services from Clapham Junction to Willesden and from Brighton to Watford, there are inter-regional workings and an immense variety of freight. On a glorious afternoon in August 1994, the Petroleum-subsector's No 37 892 *Ripple Lane* was employed between Acton Yard and the Southern Region on a 1,000-tonne stone train that had originated at Merehead Quarry in Somerset. *Author*

Right: Proportionally, very few photographs seem to be taken during the hours of darkness, and thus a large part of the railway working day goes unrecorded. Putting that situation to rights is this imposing shot at the unlikely location (in terms of Class 37s) of St Pancras. In the latter part of 1988 the 15.30FO Derby– St Pancras and 18.20 return were diagrammed for a Class 37/4, and on 21 October that year No 37 428 *David Lloyd George* was photographed on the return working, beneath the magnificent trainshed of the old Midland Railway's terminus. The giant clock shows that there are six minutes to go before departure. *Brian Morrison*

Below: Locomotive-hauled trains at Cannon Street are extremely rare. Seen from a signal gantry above the River Thames (access to which requires a trackside pass) outside the station on 23 January 2006, Nos 37 425 *Pride of the Valleys / Balchder y Cymoedd* (topping) and 37 411 *Caerphilly Castle / Castell Caerffili* (tailing) leave behind the twin turrets with a SERCo track-recording train touring South Eastern suburban lines. Having started from Hither Green, this had run via Sidcup, Bexleyheath and Greenwich and from here would head for Strood and Paddock Wood. *Brian Morrison*

North Wales

Left: In 1995 there was a shift away from Manchester–Blackpool/Southport services for a block of Class 37/4 ETH locomotives, which then found themselves allocated to Crewe for use on the Birmingham New Street–Crewe–Holyhead route. However, Class 37s had worked some North Wales services before this time; on 17 July 1993, dwarfed by the ship in the background, Regional Railways' No 37 414 *Cathays C&W Works 1846-1993* awaits the 'rightaway' from Holyhead with a train for Crewe. *Gavin Morrison*

Below: Its EWS red-and-yellow livery providing a vivid contrast with the blues and whites of the Regional Railways rolling stock forming the 1K71 morning train to Crewe, No 37 408 *Loch Rannoch* leaves Holyhead station on 17 May 1999. The Class 37s were regular performers on the route until the new Class 175 'Coradia' DMUs came on stream in the year 2000. *Gavin Morrison*

Right: Little colour film seems to be exposed when climatic conditions are atrocious; on this summer's day in June 1993 the heavens opened, and only the foolhardy continued to stand on a bridge waiting for a train! In deplorable weather, FMYT (Railfreight Metals, Thornaby) Class 37/5 No 37 509 plods its way through Rhyl station with a train of empty ballast hoppers, possibly for the loading-point at Penmaenmawr, west of Llandudno Junction. *Author*

Left: Bangor station is set in a most unusual location and nestles between two railway tunnels – Bangor Tunnel to the east and Belmont Tunnel to the west. Waiting to depart from Bangor for Holyhead with a rake of Regional Railways coaches in June 1997 is EWS Class 37/4 No 37 419. It is interesting to note that early repaints used the letters 'E W & S'; plain 'EWS' later became standard. *Author*

Right: A bleak day for rail passengers and caravanners (who no doubt wish they had gone abroad) in June 1993 as the grey sea washes the North Wales shoreline. Finding its way through Abergele & Pensarn on the down through road is No 37 421 with a Birmingham–Holyhead working. Although ETH-fitted, the locomotive has subsector markings identifying it as a Railfreight Petroleum machine, which fact merely serves to underline the class's remarkable mixed-traffic capability. *Author*

Avon Valley

Left: The diminutive halt at Avoncliffe, between Bath and Bradford-on-Avon, has platforms that are barely long enough to accommodate a single coach, but that is of no consequence to the driver or guard of this Weymouth–Bristol Temple Meads service, passing at speed in July 1994. Returning holidaymakers to the reality of everyday life, the train is headed by Regional Railways-liveried No 37 414 *Cathays C&W Works 1846-1993*, named after the now-closed facility to the north of Cardiff Central. *Author*

Below: Not all Class 37 mileage through the lovely Avon Valley is at the head of passenger trains to/from Weymouth, as there has been plenty of freight activity over the years. In the 1980s the favourite regular working for Class 37 appearances was the 03.20 Carlisle–Eastleigh, which left Severn Tunnel Junction at 16.45, but a more impressive rival in later years was stone traffic for construction of the second road bridge across the River Severn. Threading their way through the valley near Freshford in July 1994 with empties returning to the Somerset quarries are a pair of unidentified split-headcode 'Tractors' (believed to be Nos 37 038 and 37 098) in 'Dutch' yellow-and-grey Departmental livery. *Author*

The author has indelible memories of Class 37s in the Avon Valley, and many happy days were spent 'on safari', staking out these superb machines. The river has many moods, and the seasons bring different lighting and perspective values to the numerous photogenic locations. On 22 July 1995 an early start was necessary to capture No 37 412 *Driver John Elliott* at the head of the 09.00 Bristol Temple Meads–Weymouth, but this was rewarded by the sound of the English Electric 12-cylinder engine reverberating off the sides of the valley just south of Bradford-on-Avon. The locomotive is seen crossing one of the river's many weirs, with the water, a trace of exhaust and the large Transrail 'T' all demanding attention. *Author*

Coats of many colours

Above: In a fleet of more than 300 locomotives, some of which have been in service for over 45 years, it is inevitable that there should be dozens of liveries, with hundreds of minor variations, and this section depicts but a few permutations to supplement those already featured. In 2004 No 37 197 was owned by Ian Riley Engineering. Painted in Brunswick green and light grey, the impressive-looking machine is seen heading through Rotherham Masborough with a special for York on 19 June. *Gavin Morrison*

Left: Enthusiasts enjoy some rare mileage during a Scottish Railway Preservation Society railtour as EWS No 37 428, in 'Royal Scotsman' livery, runs along the freight-only Seaton-on-Tees branch to Hartlepool nuclear power station on 12 August 2000. The fence is lined by colourful cars awaiting scrapping, which make the elderly maroon Mk 1 stock look quite smart! The train originated from far-off Linlithgow, between Falkirk and Edinburgh. *Gavin Morrison*

Above: Its Warrington–Basford Hall ballast train having been diverted away from the West Coast main line due to permanent-way work, EWS No 37 411 *The Scottish Railway Preservation Society* glows in the winter sunshine of 2 December 2001 as it passes Ordsall Lane Junction, to the west of Manchester. The lines to the right lead to Salford and Pendleton, those on the left to Liverpool Road freight terminal. Note that, unusually, the locomotive has its number stencilled just below the headlight. In its career to date it has carried three different names and has latterly become a 'celebrity' locomotive (see page 102). *Gavin Morrison*

Below: A significant proposal in 1994 was the introduction of regional 'Nightstar' sleeper services to link cities such as Plymouth, Newcastle and Liverpool with destinations in Europe via the Channel Tunnel. A need for diesel locomotives was anticipated, and in readiness a dozen Class 37/5s were modified and reclassified as Class 37/6. In the novel Eurostar (UK) livery, featuring silver roundels representing the Channel Tunnel, Nos 37 601 and 37 602, separated by a generator coach, are seen on an ABB test train on the East Coast main line between York and Doncaster on 17 August 1995. *Gavin Morrison*

Yorkshire

Left: Yorkshire once comprised three Ridings, the term deriving from an ancient English word for a third. Although the Ridings were abolished in 1974 in favour of the counties of North, West and South Yorkshire, this section features a variety of scenes from the old West Riding, which now constitutes major chunks of West and South Yorkshire. There is thunder in Horbury Cutting as train 6M68, an additional 36-wagon load of cement empties from Dewsbury to Earle's sidings, Hope, heads east behind Main Line-liveried Class 37/4s Nos 37 415 and 37 419 (unofficially named 'Mt Etna' and 'Mt Pinatubo') on 21 August 1995. *Gavin Morrison*

Right: On 14 May 1984, having emerged into bright sunshine from the darkness of Elland Tunnel, on the old Lancashire & Yorkshire Railway line between Sowerby Bridge and Mirfield, Nos 37 252 and 37 160 head for Immingham with a train of tankers from Preston Docks. For many years this line was freight-only, but in recent years a passenger service has been reintroduced between Huddersfield, Halifax and Bradford. *Gavin Morrison*

Left: It is hard to believe that an installation the size of Wath Yard, on the old Great Central Railway, could be closed completely and removed from the railway map, yet, although photographed as recently as 23 September 1981, this entire scene has now been consigned to history. With the sidings on the right making a symmetrical pattern, No 37 019 pauses at the head of a long rake of HAA merry-go-round coal hoppers. Adding motive-power variety are a pair of Class 20 'Choppers'. *Les Nixon*

Right: Its train comprising only a 20-ton brake van, an unidentified Class 37 heads north past the old Midland Railway signalbox and a plethora of upper-quadrant semaphore signals at Goose Hill Junction, south of Normanton. Since this photograph was taken in the 1980s this location has changed out of all recognition and, indeed, has ceased to be a junction: the lines seen here on the left, to Cudworth and Rotherham, have been lifted, leaving only the tracks on the right from Wakefield. *Author*

Above: EWS Class 37/5 No 37 521 is seen in the vicinity of Fitzwilliam with the 6M68 11.55 Dewsbury–Earle's Sidings cement empties on 5 October 1999. The photographer has chosen a location on the Leeds–Doncaster main line where, despite the presence of overhead wires, a clutter-free view of a train can be obtained. The train will shortly branch south and travel via Rotherham and Sheffield to reach its Hope Valley destination. *Gavin Morrison*

Left: Providing a blaze of colour at Burton Salmon Junction on 15 August 2001, the 6V36 08.39 Lackenby–Llanwern steel train heads south behind Nos 37 415 in EWS livery and 37 401 *The Royal Scotsman* in Great Scottish & Western Railway 'Royal Scotsman' maroon livery. By this time Class 37-hauled freights were reducing rapidly as General Motors locomotives poured into the UK and rail-borne freight was diminishing in certain industries. *Gavin Morrison*

Right: A remarkable photograph, taken at Mill Lane Junction, just south of Bradford, on Sunday 4 August 1996. No 37 516, in Loadhaul livery but without the bodyside branding, eases an engineers' train of lifted track up the bank from Bradford Exchange station and takes the Leeds line, adjacent to the old St Dunstan's station (closed in September 1952) as No 37 711 in Railfreight Metals livery descends from the Halifax line into Bradford with another engineers' train. *Gavin Morrison*

Below: In terms of size, Park Mill Colliery at Clayton West was a modest installation. The branch that served it closed to passengers in January 1983 and to all traffic, including coal, in October of that year. The track was lifted in 1986, but since then the trackbed has been used as the basis of the 15in-gauge Kirklees Light Railway. In this visual time-warp 103-ton No 37 040, pauses in the sidings beside old brick colliery buildings while collecting the loaded wagons. Note the shunter's pole leaning on the leading wagon, and beside it the sign stating that 'British Rail locomotives must not pass this sign'. The incoming empties on the left have a brake van attached, which will be added to the outbound train. The '0000' headcode gives a clue to the date (5 August 1977), BR having abandoned the display of train headcodes on locomotives the previous year. *Gavin Morrison*

DRS

Left: Direct Rail Services is owned by the Nuclear Decommissioning Authority, parent company of British Nuclear Fuels; such is today's world of complex corporate structures! The NDA was established in 1995, and the DRS offshoot was created to provide the company with a strategic rail-transport service. Initially DRS handled only loads pertaining to the nuclear industry, but more recently it has been aggressively marketing its business to a wider audience. DRS chose a livery of dark blue with a company logo in light blue, with fairly large locomotive numbers. Seen heading south of Rugby on the West Coast main line with train 4L46, the Ditton–Purfleet containers, on 5 May 2006 are Nos 37 059 and 37 069. *Gavin Morrison*

Right: The majority of the DRS Class 37s have special marker-light clusters mounted low down on the nose. Hauling a pair of nuclear flasks from Bridgwater (Somerset) to Crewe, Nos 37 218 and 37 038 (which retains its original headcode boxes and lacks the new-style marker lights) approach Flax Bourton, near Bristol, in July 2003. Initially the main DRS depot was at Sellafield on the Cumbrian Coast, but the company now has additional facilities at Carlisle and Crewe, as well as in Scotland and the South East of England. *Rail Photoprints*

Left: The DRS company has acquired a wide range of ex-BR diesel motive power. On its shopping list have been Class 37s but also, inter alia, examples of Classes 20, 33 and 47, while more recently it has followed the lead of other freight operators in acquiring brand-new Class 66 locomotives from General Motors. The company's locomotives are now in demand with railtour organisers, as was the case on 18 March 2006, when Pathfinder Tours ran a special from Gloucester to Goole. The Chartex, powered by Nos 37 218 and 37 029, is seen near Mirfield in West Yorkshire. *Gavin Morrison*

Above: DRS now advertises a 24-hour control centre for its growing operations and engineering support throughout the rail network, but it seems not all freight flows are successful. In what was stated to be the last week of the service the 4L46 Ditton–Purfleet, headed by Nos 37 259 and 37 218 passes Ripple Lane, near Barking, in late-afternoon light on 14 June 2006. *Brian Morrison*

Right: For a week in July 2006 the SERCo test train, used to detect and record track defects, was deployed on various lines in the South East. DRS won the contract to supply motive power, and on the first day, 17 July, Class 37/6s Nos 37 609 and 37 611 were provided. Its stock fresh from a 'wash and brush-up', train 1Z14, the 09.45 from Hither Green, is seen in the Kentish countryside between Bexley and Crayford at the start of its journey via the Dartford Loop; the train was then scheduled to travel on the Crayford Spur to London Bridge via Bexleyheath before traversing a maze of other lines in South East London and Kent. *Brian Morrison*

Lincolnshire

In terms of railway traffic there are considerable differences between north and south Lincolnshire. In the south DMUs provide passenger services over rural lines running across largely flat fenland, only Boston Docks presently providing a source of freight revenue. In the north of the original county (much of which later became part of Humberside), in the Scunthorpe and Immingham areas, there are significant industrial complexes. In the good old days, when numerous locomotive-hauled trains from the Midlands and the North travelled to the seaside at Skegness on summer Saturdays, 'large logo' No 37 008 passes Hubbert's Bridge, west of Boston, with the 09.50 relief express from Grantham to Skegness. The photograph dates from 31 August 1987. *John C. Baker*

Right: This photograph from the archives demonstrates the long association of Class 37s with the lines of southern Lincolnshire. Leaving the country junction and railway crossroads of Sleaford with train 3J96, the 8.16am parcels to March, on 28 August 1964, is No D6810. The Sleaford East signalman has given the train 'the road', and, judging by the exhaust, the locomotive is under full power. Only the first 30 EE Type 3s were delivered in all-green livery; from No D6730 all locomotives were delivered with a small yellow warning panel on each nose end. *J. Madley*

Left: Back in 1974 the UK's largest flow of iron ore was that on the 23-mile route between Immingham Docks and the Santon terminal of British Steel Corporation's Appleby Frodingham Works at Scunthorpe, which saw as many as 13 trains, each comprising 21 100-tonne (gross) hopper wagons, operating daily. Before the era of modern Type 5 freight locomotives pairs of Class 37s were the staple motive power; Nos 37 271 and 37 272 are seen drawing their train under the bulk-loading facility at Immingham in 1974. *C. P. Boocock*

Right: Even after the advent of Classes 56, 58 and 60, pairs of 'Syphons' could still be seen on the iron-ore trains of north Lincolnshire. On the basis of 'what goes up must come down', Nos 37 351 and 37 381, both from Railfreight's FMYI (Metals, Immingham) subsector, are seen approaching the junction station of Barnetby on 21 March 1991 with iron-ore empties returning from Santon to Immingham. In 2007 semaphore signals survived, but their days were numbered. *Brian Morrison*

Rhymney

Left: For many years there was a special relationship between Class 37s and the Rhymney branch. Coal trains in particular would work up to Ystrad Mynach to the various collieries on the Dowlais branch, and enthusiast specials have traversed the line on many occasions. However, in 1994 then train operator Cardiff Railways introduced locomotive-hauled services at peak times between Rhymney and Cardiff, and ETH Class 37/4s duly became the standard motive power. In 2005 it was announced that these trains would end, and a special farewell weekend was held on 3/4 December. Green-liveried EWS No 37 411 *Caerphilly Castle / Castell Caerffili*, on hire to Arriva Trains Wales, arrives at Bargoed with the 14.14 Rhymney–Cardiff Central on the Saturday. *Brian Morrison*

Below: This superb view epitomises the Cardiff–Rhymney services enjoyed by commuting locals during recent years. In a livery particularly suited to the Class 37s, 'large logo' No 37 425 *Pride of the Valleys / Balchder y Cymoedd* (formerly *Sir Robert McAlpine / Concrete Bob*) rounds the curve south of Ystrad Mynach with the 11.56 Rhymney–Cardiff Central, also on 3 December 2005. The air-conditioned rolling stock is in Virgin Trains livery. Note the elevated signalbox (on the extreme left) and the delightful pair of home signals, with white backing plates to aid sighting by drivers. After all the farewells Class 37s would return to the Rhymney line in 2006! *Brian Morrison*

South Wales

Right: The surprise announcement, made in the early months of 2006, that the stabling-point at Newport, known locally as Godfrey Road, was to close helped focus the mind on its long association with Class 37s. It is almost certain that every major Class 37 livery has appeared at this location, and the first of four photographs affording a glimpse of this variety features Loadhaul-liveried Class 37/7 No 37 884 *Gartcosh*, seen on shed on 26 June 1999. *Norman E. Preedy*

Right: By contrast, on 14 February 2004, a slightly rarer bird turned up in the shape of InterCity 'Swallow'-liveried No 37 685, a repaint having been undertaken by Old Oak Common towards the end of 2003. The exhaust reveals that although the locomotive is stabled the engine is still idling. *Norman E. Preedy*

Right: Adjacent to the stabling-point but standing at the main island platform on 3 February 2001 is ex-Channel Tunnel Class 37/6 No 37 610 in DRS livery. This locomotive was a South Wales resident in times past, when it carried the number 37 181. It has since been named *The Malcolm Group*. *Norman E. Preedy*

Right: Completing this quartet of Class 37s at Newport is No 37 428, which was stabled there on 7 April 2001. The locomotive is seen in 'Royal Scotsman' maroon livery with some lining embellishment, but the elements seem to have taken their toll in terms of cleanliness. Locomotives are now stabled at the nearby Alexandra Dock Junction. *Norman E. Preedy*

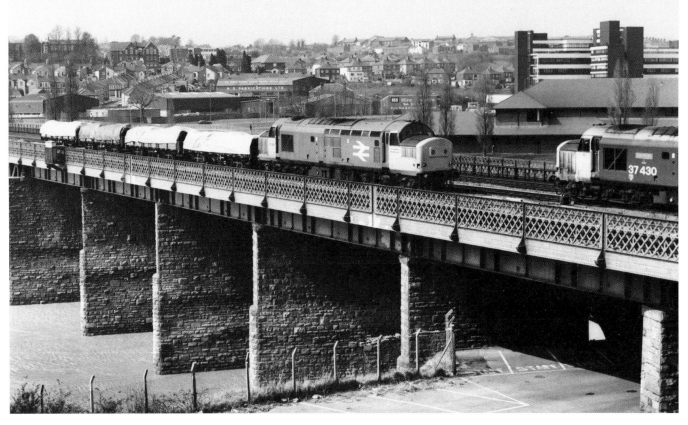

Above: A chance encounter on the railway bridge over the River Usk at Newport, Gwent in April 1988. Recorded from a public car park, 'large logo' Class 37/4 No 37 430 *Cwmbran*, arriving with a passenger train from Liverpool Lime Street to Cardiff, passes Railfreight-liveried No 37 255 in charge of a Metals-subsector working. *Author*

Below: The scale and variety of industry in South Wales produced an immense volume of rail-borne freight, and in 1980 there seemed to be a constant procession of freight trains through Newport, the only drawback for the photographer being that the succession of Class 37s were all painted in drab BR blue livery that had not seen a washer for months. However, the reality (not fully appreciated at the time) was that coal, oil, iron and steel, as well as wagonload freight, were all in steep decline. Seen passing through Newport station on 14 July with a heavy load of steel bars for reinforcing concrete structures is No 37 170. *Author*

Right: Typical South Wales coastal scenery, with the vast BP chemical works at Baglan Bay in the background, as well as the cooling towers associated with power generation, so necessary in an industrial energy-consuming area. In April 1989 No 37 142 passes Briton Ferry Yard with a down ballast working, with a 'Shark' brake van bringing up the rear. The locomotive has since been preserved and is nowadays resident on the Bodmin & Wenford Railway in Cornwall. *Author*

Right: Head-on shots are not conducive to recording locomotive numbers, hence this split-headcode Class 37 is unidentified. Seen blasting up the incline on the single-track spur at Court Sart Junction, the 'Growler'-hauled freight had originated from one of the dozens of terminals in either the Swansea Docks area or along the Swansea-avoiding line. The main line from Cardiff to Swansea is on the left. *Author*

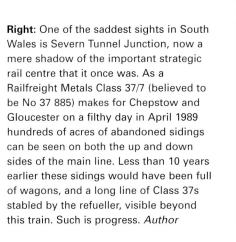

Right: One of the saddest sights in South Wales is Severn Tunnel Junction, now a mere shadow of the important strategic rail centre that it once was. As a Railfreight Metals Class 37/7 (believed to be No 37 885) makes for Chepstow and Gloucester on a filthy day in April 1989 hundreds of acres of abandoned sidings can be seen on both the up and down sides of the main line. Less than 10 years earlier these sidings would have been full of wagons, and a long line of Class 37s stabled by the refueller, visible beyond this train. Such is progress. *Author*

East Midlands

Left: The Harry Needle Railroad Co, of St Helens, Lancashire, sells itself as the UK's 'premier industrial and main-line locomotive hire and overhaul company'. It also deals with rolling-stock disposal, component recovery and site clearances. In 2003 the company acquired some Class 37 locomotives and adopted a livery of orange and grey with black lining. One of the first opportunities to show off the new paint scheme was at the Barrow Hill Open Day of 4 October 2003, when No 37 515 posed for the cameras. *Norman E. Preedy*

Right: The busy four-track section between Tapton Junction and Clay Cross Junction was a happy hunting-ground for Class 37 fans. Seen just north of Chesterfield station on a misty 4 February 1987, No 37 080 makes the switch from the Sheffield (via Dore & Totley) lines to the Staveley–Tinsley Yard route. The ballast train of vacuum-braked four-wheelers is travelling between Mountsorrel and Beighton Junction, to the east of Sheffield. *Author*

Left: On 30 May 1987, having travelled down the old Midland Railway main line through Chesterfield and Clay Cross, a Lackenby–Corby steel train headed by Nos 37 517 and 37 509 from the FMYT (Railfreight Metals, Thornaby) pool approaches Manton Junction, where it will branch off the Peterborough line to reach the Northamptonshire steelworks. Just visible in the background, to the left of the delightful (and still active) MR signalbox, is the entrance to Manton Tunnel. Sadly the entire Corby steel complex eventually closed in the 1990s. *Author*

Devon

Left: No 37 673 enjoys its moment of glory on 27 May 1989 as it pilots the 11.25 Newquay–Paddington through Dawlish station. According to the photographer both HST power cars had their engines running, so the reason for the Class 37 pilot remains a mystery; a likely explanation is a failure of the leading power car's speedometer, AWS equipment or warning horn. *P. G. Barnes*

Right: Summer Saturdays in the West Country frequently produced surprises as the insatiable demand for motive power stretched resources, resulting in freight locomotives' heading Class 1 passenger trains. On a Saturday in September 1984, to the excitement of the 'bashers' on board, what is believed to be the 08.20 Liverpool–Paignton produced a pair of 'Syphons'. The train is seen drawing into Exeter St Davids, No 37 219 leading No 37 177. The magnificent WR lower-quadrant semaphore signals would soon be history as the Exeter resignalling scheme gained pace. *Author*

Left: Every long-distance china-clay train leaving or arriving in Cornwall must traverse the county of Devon, and in recent years this commodity has produced most of the freight traffic along the former GWR main line. With a handful of sunbathers stretched out below the sea wall at Langstone Rock, near Dawlish Warren, No 37 055 heads a lightweight up air-braked Speedlink service in August 1989. The locomotive carries Railfreight Distribution decals (red diamonds on a yellow background) on its triple-grey livery, while the two vehicles immediately behind it are 80-tonne 'Tiger' wagons containing powdered china clay. *Author*

The Far North

Left: Thurso is 722 miles from London by rail, and the station is the furthest-north on Britain's rail network; nearby Wick, although not so far north, is 729 miles from the capital and 160 from Inverness. Both stations feature an overall roof built in the best traditions of branch-line termini. Seen from the buffer-stops at Thurso, Highland Rail Class 37/4 No 37 418 *An Comunn Gaidhealach* ('The Gaelic Society') will shortly return to Georgemas Junction to collect the Thurso portion of the 11.35 from Inverness. Within the station, on the left, can be seen wagons for transporting nuclear flasks to/from the 'fast breeder' reactor at Dounreay. *Gavin Morrison*

Below: In the 1970s most Far North services were worked by Sulzer-engined Type 2 locomotives, but from 1981 Class 37s were regular performers, along with various classes of DMU. However, on this occasion it was a special train that brought English Electric machinery to the Far North. The tortuous line runs near the east coast for a number of miles, but at Helmsdale it turns sharply inland. With the town's cemetery on the left and the North Sea in the background, Nos 37 428 *David Lloyd George* and 37 401 *Mary Queen of Scots* head north with the prestigious 'Orcadian' Land Cruise of 21 March 1992. *Gavin Morrison*

West Highlands

Right: In 1981 redundant Class 37s were cascaded from elsewhere in the UK and allocated to Glasgow's Eastfield depot for use on West Highland services. The Class 37 Co-Cos were far heavier than the BRCW/Sulzer Type 2s they were to replace, and it was feared that they might be too heavy for the track and bridges. However, they proved more reliable and more powerful than the Sulzers, and any concerns were soon dispelled. With mist swirling around the hills at Crianlarich on this November day in 1986 No 37 183 creeps into the station with a freight from Mossend to Fort William. The third and fourth wagons contain china clay that has travelled all the way from distant Cornwall. *Author*

Left: The '37/4' sub-class was formed during 1985/6, when 31 locomotives were refurbished and fitted with electric train heating. Of these, 17 locomotives (Nos 37 401-13/22-5) were allocated initially to Eastfield for use on the West Highland line. Although designated as passenger locomotives the '37/4s' remained available for freight use, as demonstrated here.
On 14 November 1986, embellished with Eastfield's white 'Highland Terrier' motif, No 37 412 powers away from Crianlarich with a Glasgow-bound freight that includes red-and-grey Railfreight vans. In the foreground is a line of old engineers' wagons, which look unlikely ever again to move by rail. *Author*

109

Above: This spread shows the Class 37s at their best in terms of sight (but, alas, not sound), operating amidst the West Highlands of Scotland. In the classic setting of County March Summit, 1,024ft above sea level, between Bridge of Orchy and Tyndrum Upper, the 17.50 Fort William–Euston sleepers of 14 June 1984 is powered by No 37 264, with ETHEL (Electric Train Heating Ex Locomotive) No 97 252 providing heating, lighting and air-conditioning. *Rail Photoprints*

Left: There is just a trace of snow left on the mountains as InterCity-liveried No 37 409 *Loch Awe*, of Eastfield depot, climbs away from Bridge of Orchy on 2 June 1990 with the 02.57 Carstairs–Fort William portion of the overnight sleepers from London. There was a blaze of publicity in the railway press in 2006 when, on 9 June, the last Class 37-hauled West Highland sleeper arrived in Edinburgh. However, as is often the case with 'last' workings, this was not the end, for on 30 July 2006 the booked Class 67 was not available, and train 1B01 to Euston duly departed Fort William behind No 37 406! *Rail Photoprints*

Above: In the late 1980s DMUs took over daytime West Highland services, but Class 37s continued to power sleeping-car trains and freights. Having just passed a southbound freight at Rannoch station on the other side of the viaduct, No 37 188 *Jimmy Shand* heads across Rannoch Moor with an oil train for Fort William on 18 June 1985. The 'Syphons' were ideally suited for such work but from 2005 were retired in favour of Class 66s. *Rail Photoprints*

Right: After a quarter-century of excellent service the Class 37s' reign in the West Highlands officially came to an end in mid-2006, and the sound of hard-working English Electric 12CSVT diesel engines is now but a memory. This final West Highland view, recorded on 28 June 1987, features a slightly tired-looking No 37 412 *Loch Lomond* just north of Glen Falloch with a special train from Fort William to Dufftown. The last Class 37s to work regularly on the line were Nos 37 401 and 37 405, but members of the class have continued to make occasional appearances, deputising for failed or unavailable Class 67s. *Gavin Morrison*

Acknowledgements

Locomotive type:	English Electric Type 3 Co-Co diesel-electric
Built:	1960-5 (rebuilt 1985-8)
Original numbers:	D6700-6999, D6600-8
Total number of locomotives:	309
Purpose:	Mixed traffic
Engine:	English Electric 12CSVT
	Mirrlees MB275T (Nos 37 901-4)
	Ruston RK270T (Nos 37 905/6)
Horsepower (12 CSVT engine):	1,750hp at 850rpm
Available power:	Maximum between 10mph and 79mph
Main generator (as built):	English Electric EE822/10G
Alternator (as rebuilt):	Brush BA1005A
	GEC G564AZ (Nos 37 796-803, 37 905/6)
Traction motors:	Six English Electric EE538/A
Maximum tractive effort	(Class 37/0): 55,500lb
	(Class 37/3): 56,180lb
	(Class 37/4): 57,440lb
	(Class 37/5): 55,590lb (Nos 37 501-21) or
	56,720lb (Nos 37 667-99)
	(Class 37/7): 62,680lb (Brush) or 62,580lb (GEC)
	(Class 37/9): 63,760lb (Brush) or 63,520lb (GEC)
Maximum speed:	90mph (80mph with CP7 bogies)
Fuel capacity:	830 gallons (with long-range fuel tanks: 1,689 gallons)
Boiler fuel:	120 gallons
Boiler water:	800 gallons
Weight:	102-120 tons
Length:	61ft 6in over buffers
Height:	12ft 9½in to roof panelling
Width:	8ft 10½in over panelling
Multiple coupling:	Blue Star electro-pneumatic
Route availability:	RA5 or RA7 (Classes 37/7 and 37/9)
Train heating:	Clayton RO2500/3 steam boiler (where fitted)
	electric (Class 37/4 only)

This illustrated review of Class 37 operations over a period of 45 years would not have been as comprehensive in terms of timespan, geography, train type or locomotive liveries without the assistance of a number of photographer colleagues. Many individuals, whom I also regard as friends, made special efforts to provide specific photographs and caption material. In no particular order I should like to thank Gavin Morrison, Brian Morrison, John Chalcraft (Rail Photoprints), Norman Preedy, Phil Barnes and Colin Marsden; my thanks go also to all the other photographers (whose names are credited at the end of each caption) and to the editor at Ian Allan Publishing. I further acknowledge the assistance of the publisher in allowing me access to the Ian Allan Library and in affording me freedom in terms of material selection and layout of this, my 35th book.

Please note that the copyright in respect of all monochrome negatives of the original black-and-white photographs taken by the author and included in this book belongs to Steve Davies, of 51 Eagleswell Road, Llantwit Major, Vale of Glamorgan, CF61 2UG, to whom all enquiries should be directed.

The original intention was to end this volume with a photograph of a Class 37 being cut up for scrap, but when it came to completing the book and considering the remarkable amount of work the class has done over a period of more than 45 years the author decided it was more a cause for celebration than lament. In this true 'tailpiece' view Nos 37 412 (in the distance) and 37 413 top-and-tail a train of empty 'Dogfish' ballast hoppers returning to St Blazey at the unlikely location of Coswarth Tunnel, on the Newquay branch, on Sunday, 20 March 1994. There has been no run-round facility at the seaside terminus since 1987, hence the formation. *Author*